The
Rape of Florida

Albery Whitman

LITERATURE HOUSE / GREGG PRESS
Upper Saddle River, N. J.

Republished in 1970 by
LITERATURE HOUSE
an imprint of The Gregg Press
121 Pleasant Avenue
Upper Saddle River, N. J. 07458

Standard Book Number—8398-2166-2
Library of Congress Card—71-104595

Printed in United States of America

Albery A. Whitman

TWASINTA'S SEMINOLES;

OR,

RAPE OF FLORIDA.

BY

ALBERY A. WHITMAN.

REVISED EDITION

ST. LOUIS:
NIXON-JONES PRINTING CO.
1885.

DEDICATION.

TO THE RT. REV. H. M. TURNER, D.D., LL.D.,

THIS VOLUME

IS

RESPECTFULLY INSCRIBED

BY ONE WHO

ADMIRES HIM AS A VERY NOBLE REPRESENTATIVE OF

HIS RACE.

WHITMAN.

PREFACE.

The cordial reception given the first edition of this poem by the American people, prompts me to change my former address, by adding a word to the public.

Youth thinks extravagantly and often speaks more so, but sober experience comes on to correct us. I have found that I need not quarrel and that complaining is unmanly. Going among the people for myself, I have seen that the whites have cheerfully vied with my own race in putting me before the public. Kindness is a law unto herself, and in her dominions all subjects are willing. She opens her hand with benefits, and forgets not the humble in passing. This beautiful truth has been taught me by the many who have heard my singing. The wise, the good, and great have heard me, and said that they heard a poet. And saying so much of me, an obscure young man, it causes me to hope afresh, and feel that life is worth living.

I am in active sympathy with the progressive colored man. I have a mind to think that he has a calling among his fellow-men. It may be noticed here that I use the words, colored man, instead of the word Negro. I do this because *my* feelings decide in favor of *colored* man by a vote of eight to seven. I am in active sympathy with America's *coming* colored man. I have yielded to the firm belief that he has a future. I abhor the doctrine that he is but a cipher in the world's greatness — a captive in the meshes of dominating influences. I abhor it because it is arrogantly asserted on the one hand while it is too often tacitly admitted on the other. Yet I confess that living instances of real merit *only* will correct the world's judgment and force its respect. To this end I have laid out my life. Modest enough to be patient, I am not too tame to assert that I have some hope of ultimately reaching the ears of my countrymen.

I am a colored man, and as such, I accept the situation, and enter the lists with poised lance. I disdain to whine over my " previous condition." I despise the doctrine of the *slave's allowance.* Petition and complaint are the language of imbecility and cowardice — the evidences of that puerile fear which distinguishes the soul. The time has come when all "Uncle Toms" and "Topsies" ought to die. *Goody goodness* is a sort of man worship: ignorance is its inspiration, fear its ministering spirit, and beggary its inheritance. Genius, in a right good soul, is the highest impress of the Divine Image on clay. It alone can have the respect of God and man. Dumb endurance is the stamp of heroism and mortal greatness. To it, all earth is place, all time opportunity, heaven companionship and God a friend.

As for myself, I was "bred to the plow." Amid the rugged hills, along the banks of Green River in Kentucky, I enjoyed the inestimable blessings of cabin life and hard work during the whole of my early days. I was in bondage, — *I never was a slave,* — the infamous laws of a savage despotism took my substance — what of that? Many a man has lost all he had, except his manhood. Adversity is the school of heroism, endurance the majesty of man and hope the torch of high aspirations. Acquainted with adversity, I am flattered of hope and comforted by endurance.

As to the merits of this poem, I shall not venture a word. If merit there be, it will be found. If none, palliating words will not soften criticism. I simply present Atlassa, Ewald and Palmecho, with their associates, to the public, and "bow out."

Of poetry in general, however, I will say: I am not of those "who think a poet and a bell-ringer to be equals." I do not believe poetry is on the decline. I do not believe that human advancement extinguishes the torch of sentiment. I can not think that money-getting is the whole business of man. Rather am I convinced that the world is approaching a poetical revolution. The subtle evolution of thought must yet be expressed in song. "Poesy," says one, "is the language of the imagination." Campbell said, "it is the eloquence of truth." As we understand it to-day, I think poetry is the language of universal sentiment. Torch of the unresting mind, she kindles in advance of all progress. Her waitings are on the threshold of the infinite, where, beckoning man to listen, she interprets the leaves of immortality. Her voice is the voice of Eternity dwelling in all great souls. Her aims are the inducements of heaven, and her triumphs the survival of the Beautiful, the True, and the Good. In her language there is no mistaking of that liberal thought which is the health of mind. A secret interpreter, she waits not for data, phenomena and manifestations, but anticipates and spells the wishes of Heaven.

Poesy is fair, and to her all *things* are fair: the rain prophesies, and seasons and soil give testimony that God is a friend of all His creatures, and man is His delight. In great forests she sees temples reared and hears the sounds of praise. The dumb rocks are silent, but express all real prayer.

Poesy is free, and knows not of hire. Beauty is her inspiration, — her creed is Truth, and Goodness her Divinity. The first she praises, magnifies the second, and adores the third. And to end all, in her divine right a teacher, she brings benefits even to the lowly.

Of myself in this matter, I will add : I began to *try* sayings of poetry before I knew what writing was. Before I could write a letter, I was trying to scribble down what the birds and bees and cows were saying and what even the dumb rocks were *thinking*. Nature has ever had a speech for me, and in listening to her voice, lies my satisfaction. Finally : in essaying the " stately verse," *mastered* by *only* Spenser, Byron, and a very few other great poets, I may seem to have "rushed in where angels fear to tread." To this view of the matter, I will say by way of defense : some one of my race is sure to do everything that any one else has ever done, and as none of my race have ever executed a poem in the " stately verse," I simply *venture in.*

ALBERY A. WHITMAN.

TWASINTA'S SEMINOLES; OR RAPE OF FLORIDA.

CANTO I.

INVOCATION.

I.

The poet hath a realm within, and throne,
And in his own soul singeth his lament.
A comer often in the world unknown —
A flaming minister to mortals sent;
In an apocalypse of sentiment
He shows in colors true the right or wrong,
And lights the soul of virtue with content;
Oh! could the world without him please us long?
What truth is there that lives and does not live in song?

II.

"The stuff's in him of robust manliness,
He is a poet, singing more by ear
Than note." His great heart filled with tenderness,
Thus spoke the patriarch bard of Cedarmere
Of me, who dwelt in a most obscure sphere;
For I was in the tents of bondage when
The muse inspired, and ere my song grew clear,
The graceful Bryant called his fellow-men
To mark what in my lay seemed pleasing to him then.

III.

O! shade of our departed Sire of song!
If what to us is dim be clear to thee,
Hear while my yet rude numbers flow along!
If spirit may a mortal's teacher be,
Stand thou near by and guidance offer me!
That, like thy verses, clear as summer blue, —
Bright mirrors of the peaceful and the free,
Reflecting e'er the good, the great and true, —
So mine may be, and *I* my pleasing task pursue.

IV.

Say, then, of that too soon forgotten race
That flourished once, but long has been obscure
In Florida, and where the seas embrace
The Spanish isles; say if e'er lives more pure
Warmed veins, or patriots could more endure
Around the altars of their native bourne!
Say, when their flow'ry landscapes could allure,
What peaceful seasons did to them return,
And how requited labor filled his golden urn!

V.

How sweet their little fields of golden corn!
How pleasure smiled o'er all the varying scene!
How, 'mid her dewy murmurs dreamt the morn,
As Summer lingered in the deep serene!
How nibbling flocks spread on the hillsides green,
And cattle herded in the vales below;
And how wild meadows stretched in bloom-sweet sheen,
Beneath unconquered shades, where lovers go
When comes the evening star above the dark to glow!

VI.

In this delightful valley of the isle,
Where dwelt the proud Maroon, were not deeds done
Which roused the Seminole and fierce exile
To more than savage daring? Here begun
The valiant struggles of a forest son;
And tho' by wrong's leagued numbers overborne,
His deeds of love and valor for him won
The envied wreath by heroes only worn,   [torn!
And which from manhood's brow oppression ne'er hath

I.

The negro slave by Swanee river sang;
Well-pleased he listened to his echoes ringing;
For in his heart a secret comfort sprang,
When Nature seemed to join his mournful singing.
To mem'ry's cherished objects fondly clinging;
His bosom felt the sunset's patient glow,
And spirit whispers into weird life springing,
Allured to worlds he trusted yet to know,
And lightened for awhile life's burdens here below.

II.

The drowsy dawn from many a low-built shed,
Beheld his kindred driven to their task;
Late evening saw them turn with weary tread
And painful faces back; and dost thou ask
How sang these bondmen? how their suff'rings mask?
Song is the soul of sympathy divine,
And hath an inner ray where hope may bask;
Song turns the poorest waters into wine,
Illumines exile hearts and makes their faces shine.

III.

The negro slave by Swanee river sang,
There, soon, the human hunter rode along;
And eagerly behind him came a gang
Of hounds and men, — the bondman hushed his song —
Around him came a silent, list'ning throng;
"Some runaway!" he muttered; said no more,
But sank from view the growing corn among;
And though deep pangs his wounded spirit bore,
He hushed his soul, and went on singing as before.

IV.

So fared the land where slaves were groaning yet —
Where beauty's eyes must feed the lusts of men!
'Tis as when horrid dreams we half forget,
Would then relate, and still relate again —
Ah! cold abhorrence hesitates my pen!
The heavens were sad, and hearts of men were faint;
Philanthropy implored and wept, but then
The wrong, unblushing, trampled on Restraint,
While feeble Law sat by and uttered no complaint.

V.

"Fly and be free!"   A whisper comes from heaven,
"Thy cries are heard!" the bondman's up and gone!
To grasp the dearest boon to mortals given,
He frantic flies, unaided and alone.
To him the red man's dwellings are unknown;
But he can crave the freedom of his race,
Can find his harvests in the desert sown,
And in the cypress forest's dark embrace
A pathway to his habitations safely trace.

VI.

The sable slave, from Georgia's utmost bounds,
Escapes for life into the Great Wahoo.
Here he has left afar the savage hounds
And human hunters that did late pursue;
There in the hommock darkly hid from view,
His wretched limbs are stretched awhile to rest,
Till some kind Seminole shall guide him thro'
To where by hound nor hunter more distrest,
He, in a flow'ry home, shall be the red man's guest.

VII.

If tilled profusion does not crown the view,
Nor wide-ranged farms begirt with fences spread;
The cultivated plot is well to do;
And where no slave his groaning life has led,
The songs of plenty fill the lowliest shed.
Who could wish more, when Nature, always green,
Brings forth fruit-bearing woods and fields of bread?
Wish more; where cheerful valleys bloom between, [been?
And herds browse on the hills, where winter ne'er has

VIII.

Shall high-domed mosque or steepled cathedral,
Alone, to man his native land endear?
Shall pride's palatial pomp and ease withal,
The only shrines of patriotism rear?
Oh! who can limit adoration's sphere,
Or check the inspiring currents of the soul? —
Who hush the whispers of the vernal year,
Or press the sons of freedom from their goal?
Or who from Nature wrest the mystery of control!

IX.

Plebian, Savage, Sage, or lord or fiend,
Man hath of justice and of right a cause.
Prior to all that e'er has contravened,
Or e'en to man's existence, justice was.
Right would be right amid the wreck of laws:
'Tis so, and all ordaining Nature gives
Somewhere to live, to every child she has;
She gives, and to her bosom each receives,
Inducing it to love the spot whereon it lives.

X.

Fair Florida! whose scenes could so enhance —
Could in the sweetness of the earth excel!
Wast thou the Seminole's inheritance?
Yea, it was thee he loved, and loved so well!
'Twas 'neath thy palms and pines he strove to dwell.
Not savage, but resentful to the knife,
For thee he sternly struggled — sternly fell!
Thoughtful and brave, in long uneven strife,
He held the verge of manhood mid dark hights of life.

XI.

A wild-born pride endeared him to thy soil!
Where roamed his herds without a keeper's care —
Where man knew not the pangs of slavish toil!
And where thou didst not blooming pleasures spare,
But well allotted each an ample share,
He loved to dwell: Oh! isn't the goal of life
Where man has plenty and to man is fair?
When free from avarice's pinch and strife,
Is earth not like the Eden-home of man and wife?

XII.

If earth were freed from those who buy and sell,
It soon were free from most, or *all* its ills;
For that which makes it, most of all, a hell,
Is what the stingy of purse of Fortune fills:
The man who blesses and the man who kills,
Oft have a kindred purpose after all, —
A purpose that will ring in Mammon's tills;
And that has ne'er unheeded made a call,
Since Eve and Adam trod the thistles of their Fall.

XIII.

What meant the actions of the great and good —
The Christ and His Apostles — holy men!
Why wandered they about in solitude,
Despising what the world called greatness then?
Why shun the num'rous city's places, when
Eternal themes their warning tongues inspired —
Why, but to reach Edenic source again
In nature? Why, if not that they aspired
To tarry, till seraphic touch and flame had fired

XIV.

Their hearts to work man's restoration? This,
This is the voice of Time unfolding truth!
Oh! does not Nature teach us primal bliss?
Who has not felt her lessons in his youth?
And having felt, who can forget forsooth!
The voice of birds, the toil and hum of bees,
And air all filled with sounds, sweet or uncouth,
Dark hights, majestic woods and rolling seas
Have been my teachers, and my teachers still be these!

XV.

Have I not seen the hills of Candahar
Clothed in the fury of a thunder storm,
When Majesty rolled in His cloud-dark car —
Wreathed His dread brow with lightning's livid form,
And with a deluge robed His threat'ning arm !
Not seen, when night fled His terrific feet,
The great deep rose to utter forth alarm,
The hills in dreadful hurry rushed to meet,   [seat !
And rocking mountains started from their darkened

XVI.

In happy childhood I have even loved
To sport the wild, and in the front and face
Of dreadest Nature, watch the storm unmoved,
That tore the oak tree from its ancient place
And took the hilltops in its dark embrace ;
And then I've loved the pleasing after-view —
The quiet valleys spanned with light and grace —
The watery field, replete with life anew,
And sunset robing earth in love's sublimest hue.

XVII.

Thus, when afar the wide Bahamas shone, —
In lucent stillness gleamed the sunset sea —
When day's last rim sank like a molten zone,
Emblaz'ning in Omnific heraldry
The far-off crag and latest mountain tree ;
Thus, on a stand dividing worlds I've stood,
Till, touched by the dark wand of mystery,
I felt the brow of night, and earth imbued
With dread emotions of a great eternal Good

XVIII.

Upon the shells by Carribea's wave
I've heard the anthems of the mighty sea ;
Heard there the dark pines that their voices gave,
And heard a stream denote its minstrelsy —
How sweet, *all* lonely, was it there to be !
The stars were bright, the moon was up and clear ;
But, when I thought of those who once were free,
And came at wonted times to worship there ;
The sea's deep voice grew sad and claimed of me a tear !

XIX.

Oh ! sing it in the light of freedom's morn,
Tho' tyrant wars have made the earth a grave ;
The good, the great, and true, are, if so, born,
And so with slaves, *chains do not make the slave !*
If high-souled birth be what the mother gave, —
If manly birth, and manly to the core, —
Whate'er the test, the man will he behave !
Crush him to earth and crush him o'er and o'er,
A man he'll rise at last and meet you as before.

XX.

So with our young Atlassa, hero-born, —
Free as the air within his palmy shade,
The nobler traits that do the man adorn,
In him were native : Not the music made
In Tampa's forests or the everglade
Was fitter, than in this young Seminole
Was the proud spirit which did life pervade,
And glow and tremble in his ardent soul —
Which, lit his inmost-self, and spurned all mean control.

XXI.

Than him none followed chase with nimbler feet,
None readier in the forest council rose ;
To speak for war, e'er sober and discreet,
In battle stern, but kind to fallen foes.
He led the *charge*, but halted, — slow to close
The vexed retreat: In front of battle he,
Handsome and wild his proud form would expose ;
But in the cheering van of victory,
Gentle and brave he was the real chief to see.

XXII.

Lo ! mid a thousand warriors where he stands,
Pride of all hearts and idol of his race !
Look how the chieftains of his war-tried bands
Kindle their courage in his valiant face !
And as his lips in council open, trace
How deep suspense her earnest furrows makes
On ev'ry brow ! How rings the forest-place
With sounding cheers ! when native valor wakes
His dark intrepid eyes, and he their standard takes !

XXIII.

Proud spirit of the hommock-bounded home
Well wast thy valor like a buckler worn !
And when the light of other times shall come, —
When history's muse shall venture to adorn
The brow of all her children hero-born, —
When the bold truth to man alike assigns
The place he merits, of no honor shorn ;
The wreath shall be, that thy brave front entwines,
As green as Mickasukie's everlasting pines !

XXIV.

Well bled thy warriors at their leader's side !
Well stood they the oppressor's wasting fire ;
For years sweep on, and in their noiseless tide,
Bear down the mem'ries of the past ! The dire
And gloomful works of tyrants shall expire,
Till naught survives, save truth's great victories ;
Then shall the voyager on his way aspire
To ponder what vast wrecks of time he sees,
And on Fame's temple columns read their memories !

XXV.

Not so with Osceola, thy dark mate ;
The hidden terror of the hommock, he
Sat gloomily and nursed a bitter hate, —
The white man was his common enemy —
He rubbed the burning wounds of injury,
And plotted in his dreadful silent gloom ;
As dangerous as a rock beneath the sea.
And when in fray he showed his fearless plume,
Revenge made sweet the blows that dealt the white
man's doom.

XXVI.

The pent-up wrath that rankled in his breast,
O'er smould'ring embers shot a lurid glare,
And wrongs that time itself had not redrest,
In ghost-like silence stalked and glimmered there.
And from the wizzard caverns of despair,
Came voice and groan, reminding o'er and o'er
The outrage on his wife so young and fair ;
And so, by heaven and earth and hell he swore
To treat in council with the white man never more.

XXVII.

Such were the chiefs who led their daring braves
In many a battle nobly lost or won,
And consecrated Mickasukie's graves
To that sweet province of the summer sun!
And still shall history forgetful run?
Shall legend too be mute? then Poesy,
Divinest chronicler of deeds well done,
From thy blest shrine and annals of the free,
Sing forth thy praise and man shall hear attentively

XXVIII.

The poorest negro coming to their shore,
To them was brother — their own flesh and blood, —
They sought his wretched manhood to restore, —
They found his hidings in the swampy wood,
And brought him forth — in arms before him stood, —
The citizens of God and sovran earth, —
They shot straight forward looks with flame imbued,
Till in him manhood sprang, a noble birth,
And warrior-armed he rose to all that manhood's worth.

XXIX.

On the dark front of battle often seen,
Or holding dang'rous posts through dreadful hours, —
In ranks obedient, in command serene,
His comrades learn to note the tested powers
Which prove that valor is not always ours,
Be whomsoever we: A common race
Soon from this union flows — soon rarest flowers
Bloom out and smile in beauty's blending grace,
And rivals they become for love's sublimest place.

XXX.

The native warrior leads his ebon maid,
The dark young brave his bloom-hued lover wins ;
And where soft spruce and willows mingle shade,
Young life mid sunniest hours its course begins :
All Nature pours its never-ending dins
In groves of rare-hued leaf without'n end, —
'Tis as if Time, forgetting Edén's sins,
Relents, and spirit visitors descend
In love's remembered tokens, earth once more to blend.

XXXI.

The sleepy mosses wave within the sun,
And on the dark elms climbs the mistletoe ;
Great tangled vines through pendant branches run,
And hang their purple clusters far below ;
The old pines wave their summits to and fro,
And dancing to the earth, impatient light
Touches the languid scene, to quickly go,
Like some gay spirit in its sunny plight,
That, visiting the earth, did glance and take its flight.

XXXII.

Here lapped in Sylvia's all-composing shade,
Reposed a lake beneath the thick-wood hill
Whose shady base, by night and day was made
The scene of trystings : Pining there until
The shadow crept upon the midnight sill,
The love-sick youth spoke vows unto the moon ;
And pond'ring by the waters lone and still,
The old man conned his lifetime's Afternoon,
And turned the pleasing view, " I shall be going soon.'

XXXIII.

" Come now, my love, the moon is on the lake ;
Upon the waters is my light canoe ;
Come with me, love, and gladsome oars shall make
A music on the parting wave for you, —
Come o'er the waters deep and dark and blue ;
Come where the lilies in the marge have sprung,
Come with me, love, for Oh, my love is true ! "
This is the song that on the lake was sung,
The boatman sang it over when his heart was young.

XXXIV.

The boatman's song is hushed ; the night is still,
Still as the vault of heaven, — a plashy oar
Starts from the shadows by the darkling hill,
And softly dips towards the farther shore ;
Now stops, now dips again — is heard no more.
But follow the nook by yonder tree, —
Where spouts a tiny stream with fretish roar,
His light canoe is riding noiselessly —
A Chieftain's light canoe, in which his maid you see.

XXXV.

Ah ! how her wild dark wealth of tresses spread
Below the arm that round her partly lies !
And as she leans her half reluctant head,
See how intense the glances that she tries !
Her very soul is mounting to her eyes
Lit with the fires of her proud ancestry ;
And as her chieftain hears her faint replies,
How his high spirit doth adore to see
His princess-child, the bright star of his destiny !

XXXVI.

"A maid from islands in a far, far sea,
Came to our shores, upon a day, a day;
A beauty fair, a beauty fair was she,
And took our young Chief's heart away, away;
Tho' all the world could not we heard him say.
And oh! we love our chieftain and his maid,
And so will we, and so will we for aye! "
This was the night-song on the lake delayed, —
The boatman sang it over in the willows' shade.

XXXVII.

The scout at eve to Mickasukie came;
The stories of Twasinta were his boast, —
A stately chief, Palmecho was his name,
Had numerous herds and fields, and had a host
Of servants in the vale from Tampa's coast.
A proud descendant of a House of Spain,
Distinguished as a patron, gen'rous most,
Whoever sought his roof, sought not in vain,
And he who tarried once, must shelter there again.

XXXVIII.

What if his child, of Maroon mother born,
Were not so white as fancy's *marble art?*
What if Care's tedious skill did not adorn? —
A native air did nobler charms impart;
For beauty blossomed wildly in her heart:
The rosebud's youngest tinge was in her cheek,
And her dark restless eyes could dance and start
As if the sparkling sense were wont to speak,
And hurl the insult back that woman's heart is weak.

XXXIX.

Lo! where yon age-browned mansion meets the eyes!
The brook below it winds how placidly!
A house of proud ancestral families,
How venerable is its history!
Whilom here met the sons of liberty;
The counsel and the courage of a time
When civilization, crossing o'er the sea,
Courted the perils of an unknown clime,   [sublime.
And reared the Cross of Spain to mark conquests

XL.

But of thy conquests, what remains for thee,
Except our sighs, thou proud but feeble Spain!
Thy flow'r and pride, Lisboa's chivalry,
Could not on these wild shores prolong thy reign.
For man waxed mighty and his God was Gain.
What if thy ancient mounts are castle-crowned?
What if thy vales do open to the main,
With cloisters in the distance time-embrowned?
These are but glimmerings of what was once renowned.

XLI.

Was not thy standard on these shores unfurled?—
Dominions named for thy "most Christian Queen"
The smile-provoking jest of a New World,
Whose sons in battle had victorious been,
O'er English vet'rans, who had service seen?
Yea, when the luchre-loving Saxon grew
And fattened on the blood of slaves, I ween
Not much remained for errant hands to do,
Except to seize and hold the weak in bondage too!

XLII.

But Saragossa's flash o'er war's red field,
That nerved thy sons in havoc's revelry.·
Held in young Ewald's softer glance concealed,
The dark springs of Astrusian chivalry, —
The lash-hid fires of valor's destiny —
Such eyes, the raging battle could not tame :
Yet they could shed the sweet light of a plea ;
Enkindling in love's soft consenting flame,
A pride that nobly linked with beauty's charming name.

XLIII.

But we return ;   By Carribea's shore
And Tampa far, the Maroon's race is run !
Gone are his children ; him they call no more !
No more they gather in the setting sun
To join their pastimes, after toil is done !
Pathetic silence covers with a pall
The scene which all the living seem to shun,
And something seems to whisper, after all :
" And, ah ! did such and *such* Twasinta's homes befall !"

XLIV.

Here many an exile found his long sought rest,
And built his cot in woods afar, or lane.
Warm were his greetings for the weary guest,
Who wandered thither from the distant main.
And those who came were pressed to come again.
And for what news he gathered by the way,
Of frontier happens, or of maid and swain
On foreign shores, — prolonged from day to day,
The total stranger might at will extend his stay.

XLV.

Here erst came exiles from their little farms,
To greet Palmecho and some honored guest;
Then ranged in rows, they sat with folded arms,
And heaven with rude, but fervent songs addrest :
A nameless longing kindled in each breast,
Gave soul to song, and as their voices rose,
And rolled, and echoed, dying in the West,
It seemed as if the dark hills did enclose
Unearthly choirs that chanted Nature to repose.

XLVI.

But where are they?   Their voices are no more,
Where is the proud Palmecho?   Where his child?
Ah! shall we seek them on a foreign shore,
Or follow where they wander in the wild?
Oh God! and hath our garments been defiled
With their shed blood; or what the frost and blight
That withered life where erst so sweet it smiled?
Let time's unerring finger point aright,
If Babylon be doomed, the truth should see the light.

XLVII.

Pass by their dwellings! they are desolate !
The dog has wandered there and howled and gone !
Rank weeds are growing over the broken gate,
And silence holds her dismal reign alone.
Ah! see what devastation there has done !
How o'er the scene a mournful spirit falls !
Here where a cheerful hearth whilom hast shone,
The dim mole burrows — sunken lean the walls,
And wizard voices whisper in the naked halls !

XLVIII.

Thus have we, Mickasukie, seen thy brave,
And, too, Twasinta, seen thy homes decline !
Thus have we found how yearns the poorest slave
For freedom — how at patriotism's shrine,
The ardor of the exile is divine ;
And now, that in the tide of years o'erflown,
There's scarcely left a trace of thee and thine,
We pause and sigh, mid wrecks that'time hath strewn;
Of all the world has been how little now is known !

XLIX.

The plowman's furrow marks the crumbling field,
Where all unnoticed, war's rude weapons spread ;
While neath his heedless step may lie concealed,
The strange and thrilling annals of the dead !
On some eventful day there may have bled,
Freemen as brave as Balaklava knew ;
While there may rest some glorious leader's head,
Whose matchless valor to his standard drew   [threw.
Brave hosts, who round their homes a wall of battle

L.

Oh ! would the muse of history rend the veil,
And bring her hidden instances to light ;
How many standards of the proud would trail,
As thousands all unknown would rush in sight !
From steepled vale and celebrated hight !
Wherever civilization spreads her name,
Nations that perished in the scourge and blight
Of wars would rise, and in the book of fame,
Record their struggles and their heroes' deeds proclaim.

LI.

Not Albion's will nor Scotia's price alone,
Could drum and slogan till the air should shriek
With martial praise, — nor with their lips of stone,
Could Tyber's Mistress and Illyrium speak
The godlike deeds of Roman and of Greek;
Nay, where the orange blows in yellow gold, —
Where eve is thoughtful and the morn is meek, —
Where stood the quick-eyed warrior dark and bold,
Applausing earth would hear the deeds of glory told.

LII.

Then from the lips of unforgetting time,
To hear what did Twasinta's homes befall
When war-storms overspread that peaceful clime —
To know what anguish did all hearts appall,
When separations brought death after all —
To hear how love can mortal dread unmask, —
To hear, and write at candor's earnest call,
That I may answer if mankind shall ask,
In truth — this be my aim, this be my further task.

CANTO II.

I.

The trump of fame is but the thunder's tone
Borne off forever, dying on the wind.
The glorious summits of the ages gone,
In dim remoteness scarcely lift the mind :
The mighty deeds that thrilled of yore, mankind,
Are now forgotten or but seldom told ;
Th' unresting spirit e'er the new must find —
Old lands, old tongues, old heav'ns and earths — all old
Things pass away, as time displays the new unrolled.

II.

What is there now of gods and Mikadoos,
And dukes, and lords, or other tilted things,
In this live age ? — this busy world profuse
With evolution ? — when each hour there springs
New truths, and new sensations mount their wings ?
Inherent mention's scarcely worth the pains,
The world cares little whose grand sires were kings ;
I'd rather be a squatter on the plains,
And know that I possessed industry, pluck and brains.

III.

Greatness, by nature, cannot be entailed ;
It is an office ending with the man, —
Sage, hero, Savior, tho' the Sire be hailed,
The son may reach obscurity in the van :
Sublime achievements know no patent plan,
Man's immortality's a book with seals,
And none but God shall open — none else can, —
But opened, it the mystery reveals, —
Manhood's conquest of man to heav'n's respect appeals.

IV.

Is manhood less because man's face is black ?
Let thunders of the loosened seals reply !
Who shall the rider's restive steed turn back,
Or who withstand the arrows he lets fly,
Between the mountains of eternity ?
Genius ride forth ! thou gift and torch of heav'n !
The mastery is kindled in thine eye ;
To conquest ride ! thy bow of strength is giv'n —
The trampled hordes of caste before thee shall be driv'n !

V.

Who is't would beg ? What man permission crave
To give his thoughts their scope and rightful reign ?
Let him be cursed ! a self-manacled slave !
He's a polution to the mind's domain —
A moral garbage scattered on the plain —
An execration of the world ! — God's arm
Defend not him ! Oh ! if there is disdain
To freeze the bosom's every impulse warm,
I crave it for all who to Favor's alm's house swarm.

VI.

Shall thunders ask of man what time to beat
The march of clouds ? Or oceans beg his leave
To rock their under-worlds ? In his dread seat,
Doth Blanc consider him ? When did he weave
A mantle for the hurricane, or give
The Rockies leave to hold the dying Sun ! —
Sooner all these — sooner an earthquake heave,
And sink earth back where broods oblivion,
Than God-giv'n mind submit for gyves to be put on.

VII.

'T is hard to judge if hatred of one's race,
By those who deem themselves superior-born,
Be worse than that quiesence in disgrace,
Which only merits — and *should* only — scorn!
Oh! let me see the negro, night and morn,
Pressing and fighting in, for place and power!
If he a proud escutcheon would adorn,
All earth is place — all time th' auspicious hour, [cower?
While heaven leans forth to see, oh! can he quail or

VIII.

Ah! I abhor his protest and complaint!
His pious looks and patience I despise!
He can't evade the test, disguised as saint,
The manly voice of freedom bids him rise,
And shake himself before Philistine eyes!
And, like a lion roused, no sooner than
A foe dare come, play all his energies,
And court the fray with fury if he can;
For hell itself respects a fearless manly man!

IX.

Negro, or Arab, Zulu if one choose,
Unmoved be thou reproached for all but fear!
By the unhindered waters learn to muse,
With nature's liberal voices in thy ear;
Dwell on her nobler aspects that appear,
And make companions of all one may find:
Go rove the mountain forests far and near,
And hear the laughter of the open wind;
Then ask, what earth affords like freedom of the mind!

X.

Be thine the shoulders that may bleed — not wince,
Tho' insolence in power lay on the lash.
Look retribution! court the worst nor flinch,
If thou must meet! — upon the insult gnash!
And let thy kindled courage on him flash;
For whom he can not conquer — dare not kill —
In suff'ring dumb — in manly virtues rash —
Must with respect e'en tyrant bosoms fill,
So godlike is the man who is invincible!

XI.

I never was a slave — a robber took
My substance — what of that? The *law* my rights —
And that? I still was free and had my book —
All nature. And I learned from during hights
How silence is majestic, and invites
In admiration far beholding eyes!
And heaven taught me, with her starry nights,
How deepest speech unuttered often lies,
And that Jehovah's lessons mostly he implies.

XII.

My birth-place where the scrub-wood thicket grows,
My mother bound, and daily toil my dower;
I envy not the halo title throws
Around the birth of any; place and power
May be but empty phantoms of an hour, —
For me, I find a more enduring bliss:
Rejoicing fields, green woods — the stream — the flower,
To me have speech, and born of God, are his
Interpreters, proclaiming what true greatness is.

XIII.

Where'er I roam, in all the earth abroad,
I find *this* written in the human chart:
A love of Nature is the love of God,
And love of man 's the religion of the heart.
Man's right to think, in his majestic part
In his Creator's works — to others bless —
This is the point whence god-like actions start,
And open, conscientious manliness
Is the divinest image mortals can possess.

XIV.

Almighty fairness smiling heaven portends,
In sympathy the elements have tears;
The meekest flow'rs are their Creator's friends,
The hungry raven He in patience hears;
And e'en the sparrow's wishes reach His ears!
But when He treads the tyrant in His wrath,
And to crush wrong the horn of battle rears,
The pestilence goes forth on him who hath
Transgressed, and empires fall imploring in His path.

XV.

A god-like man is fair to fellow-men,
And gentleness is native in his soul!
He sees no fault in man till forced, and then
He wonders 't were not greater. He is whole
In valor, mercy, love, and self-control.
Virtue is his religion — Liberty
His shrine — honest contentment is his goal
And sum of bliss, and his life aims to be
In nothing excellent, save that which leaves man free.

XVI.

I envy not the man whose want of brains
Supplies a roost for race-hate's filthy brood!
The little eminence his soul attains
Is more the pity when 'tis understood,
That he, perhaps, has done the best he could!
Tread not upon him just to see him squirm!
Pity, forsooth! to crawl is his best good,
And 'tis his nat'ral way, I do affirm;
So, let him crawl his fill, he is a harmless worm!

XVII.

A lovely sunset fills the evening sky,
On glorified peaks the cloud-rims slowly fade,
Till comes the darkened east on quietly
Extending o'er the earth a solemn shade!
All things are silent, save the whispers made
By drowsy pines o'er where deep solitude
Rock, cavern, hill and valley doth pervade.
Now sinks a glimmering spirit in the wood,
And the dark brow of heav'n with myst'ry is imbued!

XVIII.

How changed the hour! How sweet to be alone
In meditations! 'Bove thee sweep thy sight
O'er the unconscious world, a baldic zone
Of heavenly sapphires burns! Behind the hight
The tranquil moon appears, and peerless night
Asserts her brilliant reign! Oh! mystery,
Interpreter of yon far mansions bright,
To find what their night-cogitations be,   [thee!
My soul would mount its eager way and dwell with

XIX.

The portals of Thine upper House, O God!
Portend a kindred of their worlds to me!
O! how the coming of Thy light abroad,
Doth lift my soul adoring up to Thee!
And is it not benign that I should see?
How could my heart in disobedience sink,
While round me rolls infinite harmony,
And thou dost woo my spirit forth to think,
And wait with Thine eternal sons upon the brink!

XX.

Thou awful One! Thy willing creature hear!
Help Thou my soul in patience here to wait;
And how soe'er to me Thou dost appear,
Lead me to look towards Thine upper gate!
Thy tender goodness is to me so great,
And Thou so near me hast Thy wonders brought.
Oh! help me love Thee more in Thine estate,
And love my fellow mortal as I ought!
Then grant that I come to Thine *upper* home of thought.

XXI.

When we behold yon citizens of heaven,
Oh! why should man oppress his brother here?
How sweet to think a Father's love hath given
To man the task to beautify this sphere,
And dwell in peace upon it everywhere!
The noblest hights e'er found by angels' ken,
The grandest vistas that to them appear,
Make not celestial joys so sweet as when
They see our earth a heaven — a brotherhood of men!

XXII.

Love in the forest, — this is is now our theme —
Was like a charming spirit in the wild
Where dwelt Atlassa.   It to him did seem
That all the earth with tints of promise smiled.
And since he met Palmecho and his child,
The waves of Mickasukie sang more sweet.
The hoarse old pines did even speak more mild,
The wild flow'rs brightened in their mossy seat ;
And Ewald's whispers lingered in the wind's retreat.

XXIII.

No wonder he from forests sports should turn,
No wonder that he learned the Spanish tongue —
And to Twasinta went that he might learn :
Nor is it strange that, his rude tribes among,
The useful arts soon into being sprung.
The faithful exile in his fields was seen ;
His herds were watched and numbered old and young ;
With waving corn the valleys soon were green, [been.
And pleasant houses reared where wigwams erst had

XXIV.

The warrior's blade now rusted in his halls,
The incantations of the seer were done ;
Free hearts arose at labor's urgent calls,
And strong hands had their cheerful tasks begun :
Soon fields of plenty rose to greet the sun.
Instead of savage revels, now the feast
Of harvests was prolonged : and there was none
So proud as our young chief that wars had ceased, —
So plain is love the proof that man is not a beast.

XXV.

The faithful exile, always giv'n to boast,
In deep'ning converse with the Seminole,
Would vow, that, "in all Carolina's coast —
All Georgia — Alabama — all the whole
Wide world, there was not such a sunny soul
As that young dark-eyed angel of the West!"
Then thus his instances would he unroll:
"Just see her feet, her hands, her timid breast, [rest!"
Her mouth, her hair — but oh! her dark eyes never

XXVI.

The Seminole would nod his gruff assent,
And long and stout they shook each other's hands.
The "queen of blossoms" was the name that went
The rounds of all the Mickasukie bands.
Ewald was princess of the sunny lands;
And as from lip to lip her mention ran,
Atlassa's inward promise to his hands,
Was valiant deeds and glory in the van, —
So sure does love inspire the manliness of man.

XXVII.

Ewald the idol of Twasinta's shades, —
Palmecho's pride and jewel of his care,
Well loved her chieftain of the everglades:
The matchless watcher of the forests fair.
As free as pine-watched Tampa's breezy air,
The head and boast of his intrepid race,
His brow was noble, — valor's seat was there —
His mien was princely and the eye could trace
The warrior-soul that warmed his wildly handsome face.

XXVIII.

Till stars were out, Ewald stood half afraid —
Half conscious of the hour — nor till the moon
Was in the misty vale, could she persuade
Herself that her young chief must not come soon :
'Twas when the whip-poor-will's loud wizard tune
Had warned her from the brake, that she could leave
Turning to go, — then pausing to commune
With shadowy thoughts, that fancy's touch did weave
Into a spell-like hope that she *might* him receive.

XXIX.

And now she heard Twasinta's watchdogs bark
At many a drowsy cotter's distant door,
Baying such sounds as travel after dark,
Leaving the after-stillness stilly more.
Thus are we warned by dogs, some say, before
Eventful times, — whether this doth reveal,
Or not, some mystery in canine lore, —
The dog's unwonted barking's apt to steal
O'er us at night, and make us strange misgivings feel.

XXX.

The very air uneasily did creep
Among the maples darkling over-head ;
And as she reached her gateway on the steep,
She found Palmecho, prying out, who said :
" There's wrong abroad, my Ewald, something dread
Is sure to happen ; " and while yet he spake
A hasty footman from the forests sped —
It was an exile, who his way did make
Straight to Palmecho, some alarming news to break.

XXXI.

As Ewald passed, she heard Atlassa's name.
Wide thro' Twasinta spread the hasty news,
Like stubbles crackling in a wind-swept flame.
Ah! now was trouble's sombre currents loose!
With muttered threats and presages profuse,
The young men's speeches stirred the eager crowd;
Whilst old men thought up their ancestral views,
And triumphs, that well made the warrior proud —
But all for action were unanimous and loud.

XXXII.

At daybreak, ere a flock fresh scatt'ring browsed
The still gray slopes, the loud echoing horn,
With sudden 'larum, all Twasinta roused;
And quietude was in her bosom torn!
How dreadful was confusion on that morn!
Soon forth from early field and drowsy cot,
Palmecho's servants, mutt'ring wrath or scorn,
O'er fence and ditches hurried to the spot
Whence came the signals, to repel a dastard plot!

XXXIII.

Hoe, axe and pick were clashing on the air,
Old swords and muskets, made by long disuse
And ancient rust to look grim things, were there!
Club, scythe and rake — whatever one might choose,
In one commingling torrent now were loose!
It was a ghastly sea, whose surge pressed surge,
All ploughed to frothy anger by abuse,
That now did roar! and on the sudden verge
Of desperation men stood nerved the worst to urge!

XXXIV.

Behind them were their homes, wives, children — all !
Forth in the breach, sons, husbands, fathers stood
To meet what came if e'en the heav'ns must fall!
Thro' unpolluted fields by Waxe's flood,
O'er meadows sweet and in the palmy wood,
The armor of the foe gleamed in the sun :
Proud was the aged maroon's incensed mood,
As forth to meet them in a feeble run,
He waved his servants back, and thus his speech begun :

XXXV.

" What troop is this that comes to mine abode ?
What seek ye here ?   Intruders ! will ye dare
To hoof my grounds ?   Why shun yon open road ?
Age quencheth not resentment ! and beware,
Whoe'er ye be, or whence soe,er ye are,
Ye come no further ! "   Rapid gestures told
How he was moved ; but without heed or care,
On rode the soldiers till he had seized hold
One's reins, and felt a sabre's blow that laid him cold.

XXXVI.

The mutt'ring breaks ! — a yell ! — a rush ! — a rage !
The servants come ! blades clatter, missiles fly !
The trained dragoons in battle-form engage
These rude, brave fellows, — aim with deadly eye —
Fall back in line, reload and deadlier try
Successive aims ! — ah ! but the gods inspire
The freeman who sees freemen by him die ! —
Each soldier's shot but builds the unconquered fire,
Twasinta's sons come on to rescue or expire !

XXXVII.

Around their prostrate chieftain they contend,
The foe's dread volleys can not hinder more!
In strong arms seized, their bleeding father-friend
Is borne away, as from the mansion door
Flies a sweet form, in frantic fondness o'er
Her sire to bend! But hark! what mean the cries
That startle silent Waxe's utmost shore?
With bated breath full soon each dragoon eyes
His rear, faces about, puts spurs, and headlong flies.

XXXVIII.

Atlassa's feerless plume was now in sight,
His Seminoles towards Twasinta cheered.
Twasinta answered with her valiant might.
And deaf'ning shouts did greet them as they neared!
Till on Palmecho's threshold they appeared,
The tempest of rejoicings held its sway;
Then on the roof the flag of Spain was reared,
And Mickasukie's braves the live-long day,
Were thro' Twasinta led in many a festive way.

XXXIX.

Did bivouac fires e'er shed a holier light
O'er the eternal slumbers of the slain,
Tho' kings were conquered, than was seen that night,
From candles burning in Twasinta's plain?
Or where the hearth-fire kindled hope again?
Roll the loud drum! and fill the brazen blast!
Heralds report the laureled victor's train! —
Let royal cups to valor's lips be past,
And still Twasinta's sons their undimmed glory hast.

XL.

Of how Atlassa's hours that night went by,
As he with Ewald watched his aged friend,
There's none mote ask, for none mote aim to pry
In sacred things, — the eye would e'en offend
If it should touch them! — angels might not bend
In admiration, or they must desire
A mortal hour or two on earth to spend:
So let us leave the mansion, nor aspire
To feast a curious gaze whence angels should retire.

XLI.

Oh! what a change one fleeting hour may bring!
What grand achievements may escape the hand,
When man had seemed to vanquish everything!
Fate, stern Dictatress, but assumes her wand
And wizard throne! — the doomed on sea and land
Doth fall by her irrevocable thrust!
The King descends to beg at her command,
The pride of empire humbles in the dust,
And all hat man *would* be bows down to what he *must*.

XLII.

She waves in air, — unreefs the tempest's shrouds!
She throws a spark, — red, angry flame forth flies
And climbs the palace dome into the clouds,
To melt in ruins the toil of centuries!
Lo! where yon sea-watched mountains darkly rise!
She thrusts them in their rock-seamed armor brown;
Volcano leaps to the night-glaring skies,
An earthquake drinks the crumbling city down,
And dashed on high the monster wrecks of Ocean frown

XLIII.

Vain mortals we! fond worms! how slow to note!
Man is but man! The subjects at his feet
To-day may aim to-morrow at his throat.
Before whom he, in open battle beat
An hour ago, *this* hour he may retreat;
Or on his armored hight-invincible
He may fall by the cunning of deceit.
From first to last, in spite of human will,
Fate ever moves unfoiled, Dictatress stern and still.

XLIV.

Fate comes at last, no telling where nor when!
The flag of truce from San Augustine's gate,
And oily speeches of designing men,
Reduced Twasinta's sons in their estate! —
Palmecho, at the council table sate
To prove by word what they in arms had claimed,
The right to live as freemen, small and great —
But, be it said, and * * * * * dust be blamed;
This land should blush whene'er a flag of truce is named.

XLV.

Palmecho spoke of wars, and rights, and lands,
The hardened pirates * * * * * at their head,
Heard with deep ire the brave old chief's demands!
With inborn hate they gave him chains instead,
And forth to seize his daughter hotly sped;
But mounting for the wilds, her valiant steed
Swept where the whist'ling cypress darkly spread,
And bore from sight in his pursuers' lead,
Foaming the scornful boast, that Ewald should be freed.

XLVI.

'Tis night, the gathering storm approaches fast;
Dark roll the low'ring clouds o'er Tampa's flood:
Earth groans as thunders utter forth their blast,
And light'nings gleam athwart the trembling wood!
'Tis as if Terror, calling up her brood,
Did howl to hear their deep responsive howls;
Or Darkness from her nether caverns stood,
To horrify with most unmortal scowls
And glints the habitations of unhappy souls!

XLVII.

Ah! such a night! How pallid nature reels
And shudders in the face of what forebodes!
And flying at Destruction's furious wheels
The wrath and pennons of insatiate gods
Now seem to rush! 'Tis still! And now the floods
Of heav'n break up! The big drops spatt'ring break!
Down! down! the sluices pour! The drenchy roads
Are streams of sheety flame! The pine tops quake
And howl in direful hubbub as the winds awake!

XLVIII.

Ah! such a night! And who is this abroad?
Lo! Where 'mid Tampa's pines she darts along!
Unreigned her fiery courser spurns the road,
And leaps away the crashing trees among!
Oh! can Ewald, so innocent and young,
Thus like a spirit of the storm fly on!
Ah! but the heart of gentleness is strong
When woman sallies forth, unhelped, alone,
With but one star of hope, and that one almost gone

XLIX.

To where a hunter's lodge gleams thro' the trees,
She turns her champing steed and hails outright;
A warrior answering in the door she sees, —
" Who's this abroad in such a stormy night ? "
She answers not, but straightway doth alight,
And when her quick eyes and Atlassa's meet,
He stands with stark amazement, speechless quite.
"'Tis I, Atlassa," now with accents sweet,   [beat.
The trembling Ewald speaks, as swift her heart doth

L.

They enter, and the chieftain lowly bows, —
He leads Ewald and quickly draws a seat;
His warriors sit around in silent rows,
And on their camp skins draw away their feet,
While their brave eyes in secret wonder meet;
Till thus to speak began their lovely guest;
They knew her language and her words were sweet —
" Warriors, I come to you with what, expressed,
Will cause a rankling fire to burn a valiant breast."

LI.

"At San Augustine *now* Palmecho pines, —
They chained him at the council there to-day!
The dungeon's gloom his aged sight confines,
I saw the arm'd men dragging him away!
'*Seize* now his child!' I heard a grim voice say,
And but for my brave steed that bore me here,
I too had been in chains, a prisoner — nay,
Had been the mock and jests of wild beasts, where,
To bear man's wrongs were death, and tenfold more
    severe."

LII.

Where glared the camp fire, now Atlassa rose, —
His oft-tried warriors waited his command.
A downward glance on these he sternly throws, —
They seize their arms and close around him stand!
Dangers ne'er bristled round a braver band!
Half list'ning, as for foes, the chief begun,
While tenderly he held young Ewald's hand:
"Witness, ye braves, who oft have battles won, —
Speak now! what peril did Atlassa ever shun?"

LIII.

"Witness, ye pines on Mickasukie's shore!
Witness, ye brakes and glens of Florida!
Did ever I disgrace the soil that bore
My race, by coward's act?   From Tampa Bay,
Have I not met the armed foe in the way,
E'en to these bounds?   Ye Seminoles once brave —
Brave ever! witness that I now do say:
Let not my country owe me e'en a grave,
If Sire Palmecho pine one fortnight more a slave!"

LIV.

Ewald now from her neck toss'd tresses wild,
And gazed upon her chieftain's valiant face —
Hope lit the spirit of the woman-child!
While with the native courage of his race,
A warrior pluck'd his chief's knife from its place,
And waving it aloft, stern-looking, cried:
"Who wears this blade and doth the task embrace
To free Palmecho, weal or woe betide,
I'll follow where he goes or perish at his side!"

LV.

Loud rang the shouts; the storm heard and the night,
The Seminole, the dread of Tampa's coast,
Was in his bosom stirred! and in such might,
Not Buena Vistas' hero, Mexic's boast,
Nor war-worn Clinch's mercenary host
Could drive him back: " She is our native star!"
They cried and yelled, for who should yell the most;
" Her beauty shines on us from Candahar,
Lead us to bring Palmecho to his home afar!"

LVI.

Atlassa spoke: "At morn bring up her steed,
And lead her to our village by the lake:
The haughty foe a cougar's cry may heed,
And cow'r ere yet the glinted morn shall wake!
Loud! loud till then, and dark, thou tempest, break!
Rock San Augustine's sentry in his sleep
Till I shall come!" He paused, adieu to take,
And out into the pitchy woods did leap,
While at his heels two braves their stormy way did keep.

LVII.

How passing strange is love! His airy wing,
Soft as gossamer, may rest on a beam,
Or glow in summer mists! Hé haunts the spring,
Gay in the ripplings of the sunbright stream!
He revels daylong in a rain show'r's dream,
And is a truant 'mid the lisping leaves.
On languid mosses where the young flow'rs teem,
A garland for his fairy mate he weaves,
And hears such elfin strains as no dull ear receives.

LVIII.

Ah! yet how strange is love!   He tunes his shell
To breathing violets, and to the show'r,
He says sweet things in song; his whispers dwell
Upon the wind's lips — he smiles in each flow'r,
Laughs in the joyous rustle of the bow'r,
And murmurs where the breezeless willows pine;
He chirrups in the morning's dew-fresh hour,
Deep in the lulled shade flees the midday shine,
And like a spell pervades the evening's gray decline.

LIX.

How passing strange!   He climbs the awful steep
To sit upon the bald old eagle's hight, —
Goes down for treasures in the corralled deep —
Disputes the reign of tempest-brooding night,
Quenches the flames of war, — nor famine's blight,
Nor burning Equinox,.nor Arctic cold,
Can stay him in his universal might!
Stranger than life, a gentle prince and bold,
In lovely woman's eyes his palace you behold.

LX.

He is capricious, often seizing hearts
That least suspect him, and as often he
Doth sport with trials — whence his sudden starts,
Hair breadth escapes, and bouts in which to be,
Not always seems most wise to chastity.
In passionate momentary wanderings,
Or long consistent quiets, ever free, —
Sweet welcome spirit, where he rests his wings,
Divinest charms invest the commonest of things!

LXI.

If now the bright sensation of an hour,
He flits from scene to scene in gorgeous hues,
Soon o'er his bloom-sweet task his wings will low'r,
And he with busy hopes content, will choose
To taste the sweets of toil-inducing dews;
And fail at last, or blossom with success,
His task is sweet, and he cannot refuse.
Thrice blessed himself, his mission is to bless —
And iron-visaged fate will smile in his caress.

LXII.

I pity him who ne'er has loved a woman,
And that outright, — with all her faults thrown in;
For the sole reason is, that he is no man,
And wears the downcast of orig'nal sin!
Who cannot look in woman's eyes, and win
That glimpse of heaven that Adam erst derived
From dwelling near enough to see within?
Love's just the Eden of which he's deprived,
Who has not truly loved, has never truly lived.

LXIII.

A hunter's lodge in Tampa's woods at night, —
A raging storm abroad — Palmecho chained —
And still where gleamed the hearth's uncertain light,
Ewald felt something in her heart which pained,
Both when it left her and when it remained:
Vacant she gazed, forgetting to forget;
Thoughts light as failing shadows were retained, —
She shut them out — they toyed with her yet, —
Such is the fate of those who toil in young love's net.

LXIV.

'Twas true, Atlassa's fame was greatly known,
His deeds of valor thrilled on many a tongue ;
Palmecho proudly did his friendship own ;
He knew the father — *then* the son was young —
He too was mighty, — valiant men among —
Yes, *he* had trained his only, gifted son,
Whose name of late in every council rung ;
She thought all this, and now again begun
Thinking of him — no — herself — no, not any one !

LXV.

A father held in chains ! She thought of that,
But he would be soon rescued, oh ! the thought !
To San Augustine, he who faltered at
No mortal peril, soon must come or ought.
Her father home again in triumph brought !
To think ! song ! music ! dance and faces bright !
Greetings, and love unhindered and untaught !
All this went in her mind, as at the light
She blindly gazed, forgetting that the night was night.

LXVI.

Now while her friends sit round to watch and guard,
We leave her with them and her thoughts to stay.
Fierce o'er the parapets the lightenings glared
At San Augustine — dangerous the way,
For, in their drowsy tents an army lay !
Atlassa crept towards a grizly tow'r,
Where is the storied prison, old and gray ;
Louder the tempest roared in that grim hour, [low'r !
And rolled the sea to meet the heav'n that seem'd to

LXVII.

Dark rose the walls, a church and prison joined,
Their kindred glooms to blend and intermix.
Dungeon'd in one, the unknown victim pined,
And in the other mid quaint candlesticks,
Sombre and weird arose a crucifix :
How fitly these portrayed the men who built
A house of God o'ershadowed by old Nick's —
Vain man, to thus offend thy Maker! wilt
Thou look on images to take away thy guilt !

LXVIII.

How slight the transit superstition makes
From common crime to acts of righteousness !
E'en human life in willful hate she takes,
Makes earth a waste and desert of distress,
Where lust and rapine rival in excess ;
Then from the smoke of some mysterious rite,
She shadows forth in all as if to bless !
And whose disputes must perish in her sight,
.An heretic, an enemy of God and right !

LXIX.

Man will hold some religion, most believe,
Mainly to hush the soul's rebuke of wrong ;
They would their very conscious selves deceive,
By hearing God's will in an unknown tongue,
And recitals not understood and long.
Hence, from the conscience, they with ease appeal
To crime's high court, the mysteries among.
What then are human hearts? — earth's woe or weal
When man wrongs man, inspired divinely *not* to *feel*

LXX.

Thus envy's blist'rous tongue her victim smites,
Malice her bludgeon whirls, Theft stalks abroad,
Lust thrives, and like a deadly serpent bites,
And highway vandalism takes the road
To spoil the earth and preach the word of God!
Oh! infamous insult to heaven and earth!
Well was the ground on Sin's account called Nod!
The sum of crimes that have *religious* birth   [dearth
Would blight the hills of God and smite them with a

LXXI.

Thus, San Augustine's church and prison joined,
Fitly portrayed crime's eminent success;
When hounds and murderous troops were loosed to find
The unsuspecting exile, and to press
The wretched Seminole from his recess
In hommock far, or by the dark bayou;
To burn his corn-fields in the wilderness,
And drag the helpless child and mother, thro'
Infested swamps to die in chains as felons do.

LXXII.

Start not! the church and prison are our text.
The Seminole and exile far removed
From busier scenes, led harmless lives, unvexed
And unmolested mid the groves they loved;
Till proud Columbia for all time proved
How much her high religion could perform,
When her slave-holding sons were truly moved! —
How soon her pious bosom could grow warm,
When heathen tribes submitted to her cruel arm.

LXXIII.

If e'er the muse of hist'ry sits to write,
And Florida appear upon her page,
This nation's crimes will blush the noonday light,
And * * * * * * 's name will lead her criminal age !
Of all the cruel wars she e'er did wage,
The cruelest will be to him assigned !
The hardened soldier's lust, the bloodhound's rage,
And San Augustine's church and prison joined,
Will be fit monuments for his chivalric mind !

LXXIV.

Extermination was his highest creed,
Bondage the *one* provision of his will,
The blood of innocence marred not the deed,
He knew no art of warfare but to kill :
Slaying was sweet, but slaughter sweeter still !
A human monster, traced thro' tears and blood
From Blount's poor fort on Apalachi's hill,
To Tampa's waters and the Mexic flood, —
But, to forget him, is, perhaps a common good !

LXXV.

Heard ye not in the cypress come a troop ?
Saw ye not by the gray old battlement,
In fear's deep anguish hurdled exiles stoop ;
Wife, mother, child within the stockade pent,
As down the angry Apalachi went
The steamy monitor, to belch out death,
While savage Creeks rushed thro' the bloody rent
Made by the iron havoc of its breath,
To massacre the wounded that did shriek beneath ?

LXXVI.

A sense of wrong burned in Atlassa's veins,
Flowed with his life, and like a fever eat;
No coward's act upon his hands left stains;
He hated e'en the likeness of deceit, —
In equal contest he knew no defeat —
The one brave object of incessant raids,
E'en Taylor's vet'rans from him must retreat;
So fierce he stood in Mickasukie's shades,
The invincible watcher of the everglades!

LXXVII.

But, on he fares beneath the prison walls,
The gates are shut, and stoutly barred the door;
A drowsy sent'nel slumbers in the halls,
And growls a snarlish cur upon the floor.
Quickly Atlassa scans the building o'er,
Locates each striking object, and discerns
How best to lead assault, and leaves before
A soldier of his daring venture learns;
Leaps from the walls and to his waiting braves returns.

LXXVIII.

O'er San Augustine's gloomy turrets rose
Serenest morn, — forth from a brilliant rift,
Where barring clouds till now the east did close,
The bright sun shone.   Vapors began to drift
Along the valleys, and from forest lift
Their mantling mists.   Refreshed the wide earth woke,
And to her joyous hosts renewed the gift
Of song and vigor: field and woodlawn spoke, [broke.
And rousing drums anon, the camp's deep slumbers

LXXIX.

The busy tents below the chieftain stirred,
The troops were seen towards a centre come ;
And now the officers' clear calls he heard, —
The soldiers' hurrying tread — the rattling drum —
The " halt" the " forward! " slow, the hush ! the hum —
The rush ! the roar ! the " double-quick," and then
The call, the count, the handling wearisome
Of arms, and now the " double-quick ! " again —
And wondered if by this they multiplied their men !

LXXX.

Forth rode the troopers in the rising sun,
To march against some unsuspecting town.
Atlassa saw them — idly chatting on, —
Bright gleamed their armor, as they sauntered down
The sedgy slope with boxwood overgrown.
Far on their way his eager eye pursued ;
The pent up fires that with his life had flown,
Now flamed anew, and as he gazing stood ;
Deep in his soul he would have met them if he could.

LXXXI.

Soon from the gates of San Augustine, he
Spied water carriers making for a brook
Beneath a copse — their guards were only three.
He knew Palmecho by his high-born look ;
This was his time ! — forth from his thick-wood nook,
Covered by under-brush, he crept around,
And near the stream a fair position took, —
Thee rifle shots loud o'er the fort did sound,   [found.
And by the sallying squads the three dead guards were

LXXXII.

No tidings were at Mickasukie heard
Of Ewald or her guards, at late nightfall.
Atlassa with his rescued friend appeared,
But joy was mute — a deep dread did enthrall,
And painful apprehensions trouble all.
Unuttered anguish settled like a spell
That e'en the oldest warriors did appall.
" Lost ! " was the whisper that on some hearts fell,
And " carried off ! " to others was a dismal knell !

LXXXIII.

Next morn Atlassa and his daring band
Are in Twasinta, yet no tidings come.
At noon they wait — till nightfall is at hand,
Still, still they hope that Ewald may come home.
Suspense yet deepens, — still they look for some
Unprobable relief ! Palmecho's groans
Begin, and anguish is no longer dumb !
Among his friends he breaks in bitter moans,
And like a hopeless child laments in falt'ring tones.

LXXXIV.

Atlassa looks upon his aged friend,
But can not speak, for words are empty now !
Straight'ning to all his hight, he will not bend,
For valor sits enthroned upon his brow, —
Ready to strike, he knows not where nor how !
So stands a lion when a foe he hears,
Knitting his nerves to deal the fatal blow :
Alarmed not that a dreadful struggle nears,
But furious to meet who stealthily appears.

LXXXV.

Not long he stood; thrice strode he in the halls,
So lately made the scenes of loud despair.
Now to his braves in undertones he calls, —
They hear but answer not, — with utmost care,
He seems to counsel and his aims declare.
They act assent! they seize their arms! they rise!
The signal giv'n, a war-whoop rends the air!
Back to his clans the Seminole now flies,
And far and near the forest answers to his cries!

LXXXVI.

"My tears are for thee, Ewald! Oh! my tears!
My cheeks do drink them as the parching sod
Drinks up the rain! How joyless now my years!
My head is low! Ah! doth this heavy rod
Chastise me to more perfect trust in God?
Else why, my sweet child, art thou gone from me!
But, if my future must in thorns be trod,
I'll gird my loins about with strength, and be
Faithful till death, and trust my Ewald yet to see!"

LXXXVII.

"On many hills my herded cattle feed,
My flocks are fair to see; and as for gold,
It falleth never to my lot to need.
My maids sing to me, and my young men hold
Their peace if I pass by! Now, as of old,
My lands do drop with fatness! — yet, have I
E'er taken ought and not restored four-fold?
Have I not filled the empty? If the cry
Of any widow came to me, drew I not nigh?"

LXXXVIII.

"What have *I* coveted?   What *have* I craved?
Fame, length of years, or glitt'ring hoarded pounds?
Is God not reconciled, am I not saved
In my Redeemer's all-atoning wounds?
If sin aboundeth, grace much more abounds!
Why, then, my broken spirit, art thou cast
A fruitless branch? a waste on barren grounds?
Ah! when the summertide of life is past,
Why am I left to grieve and linger on at last!"

LXXXIX.

" My Ewald was a young roe by the brook
Of a well upon the mountains! She stood
In quiet places by the rocks; she took
Alarm at winds in the leaves of the wood,
And shrank backwards, she was so shy! she could
Lie down on beds of violets, and they
Rose after her! — the lilies of the flood
By Candahar did love her! In the way   [stay."
From Tampa and the sea 'mong sweet shrubs was her

XC.

" My Ewald, oh! my young roe! how the shades
Of thy Twasinta mourn! Disconsolate
Are all her dwellings! Eve returns, and fades
The twilight on the hills! but at the gate
Beneath the elms, no more do congregate
Our maids and young men! our old men call thee,
But them thou answer'st not, until their weight
Of grief, by reason of their years, can be
No longer borne! The matron's eyes are tearful — she

XCI.

"In silence waits, thou comest not, and still
Her look is for thy coming! Dumb is mirth!
The valleys sing not — hushed is the sad hill!
The windows are darkened — by the dim hearth
Our eyes have run down till there is a dearth
Of tears! Without thee, Ewald, my young roe!
How comfortless is all the bitter earth!
Ah! whither gone my child! canst thou not know!
How thy Twasinta pineth! how her head is low!

XCII.

"The windows of high thought, were thy two eyes,
So large, dark and compelling! Thy fair breasts
Were even domes that did so gradual rise
O'er shrines of love! The shade at noon, that rests
On Waxe's cliffs, is thy dark brow. The vests
Of some sweet nun, loose-falling down, thy hair!
Thy voice was like the turtle's of the nests,
Thy step was as the flow'ret-pressing air; —
Thou idol of my love, my Ewald young and fair!

XCIII.

Lamenting thus, up rose the old Maroon,
Like Abraham, "with servanis," and went out,
Not knowing whither! Till the pensive moon
Was set, and darkness like a pall, about
Him fell, he pressed his strange and dismal route.
Then tenting in a wilderness unknown,
By those whose eyes were quick and arms were stout,
Securely watched, awearied he lay down,
In prayer and bitter meditations all alone!

CANTO III.

I.

On Tampa's hights gray rose the battlements:
A summer's day had gone out in the west;
The conflagration in the elements
Was ended, and the quiet shades of rest
Sank like a dreamer's visions on the breast
Of far reposing nature. Soft the hour
Was, brooding on the bay, and gently prest
And smoothed its bosom, as with magic power,
And fragrance there did breathe from many a wind-
    kissed flow'r.

II.

Ewald before her prison window sate
And leaned her face against the iron bar.
The pensive winds around her seemed to wait,
As o'er Twasinta, beaming out afar,
Beyond the dusk, she saw the evening star!
With friendly gleam, it dropped a ray of cheer,
And seemed to wait for her on Candahar!
And when it beckoned last to disappear,
She felt her eyes grow dim, and brushed away a tear.

III.

She saw the sentry pass with silent feet,
And heard the waters lisping to the shore.
Anon the muffled drums began to beat,
And moving throngs commenced a sullen roar, —
It was the sound of captives driv'n before
The troops! There husbands, wives and little ones,
To look upon Twasinta's fields no more,
Were hurried off. She heard their bitter moans,
And clanking chains that mingled with their rising
    groans!

IV.

The ship was waiting on the busy tide,
Palmecho's faithful friends must soon be gone,
And in her living tomb Ewald must bide
The stony silence of her fate alone!
Ah! how was her young bosom then undone!
'Twere better that her wretched friends might be
Where she might hear, at least, a kindred groan;
But all was over, and the sullen sea
Rolled on as ever, — an unfathomed mystery!

V.

There is a grateful balm for weeping eyes!
And e'en when trouble's little rest has flown,
Slumber, at vision's tender portals, tries
To shut the fevered lids forgetful down!
Happy the soul whose rest can find a stone,
If gentle slumber shut the aching breast!
Ewald across her wretched couch had thrown
Herself, and closed her eyes in childish rest —
Young innocence so sweet could not be long unblest!

VI.

Ah! did she dream! for still her natal star,
Above the valleys shed a lingering ray,
And seemed to wait for her on Candahar!
Once more it was the close of gentle day;
A spirit brooded in the hilltops gray,
And in the dusk were mellow sounds abroad!
Up from the solemn woods and far away,
The cheerful lab'rer from his maize fields strode,
And lads were driving home their cattle in the road.

VII.

The darkling elms were leaning o'er her gate,
Like keepers of some ancient secret still! —
She stood beneath them, half afraid to wait;
Heard lazy bells come moping from the hill,
And heard the witch-complaining whip-poor-will.
Ah! did she dream! the glow-worm's tiny glare
Was in the dews! she felt a nameless thrill,
And breath — warm flushes in the pulsing air,
Mid sweetest scent of fields and gardens blossom'd fair.

VIII.

Ah! innocence and beauty! at thy age,
To see thee slumb'ring there in such a place, —
A lovely dreamer in a human cage!
The entranced moon is looking in thy face, —
On thy half-conscious lips, she now doth trace
The quiv'rings of young pleasure's soft delight;
Such as zephyrus wakes as she doth race
With tiniest waves; or such as sunbeams bright
'Mid wild'ring toil of leaves are to the ravished sight!

IX.

Twasinta, oh Twasinta! couldst thou see,
Thro' tears, thou now wouldst look upon thy child,
As here she innocently dreams of thee!
Her shy feet press thy meadows undefiled,
'Mid first-born dews! Her heart is gay and wild
In sweet unconsciousness of what impends, —
She hears thy lulling boughs and voices mild,
As o'er her native flow'rs once more she bends! —
But where the spoiler lurks, how soon the bliss-dream
    ends!

X.

Of creeping things, there's none so vile, or worse
Than man, when he, the creature of his lusts,
Bred in the kennel of Satanic force,
Is woman's lord. Never Brazilian dusts
Were marked by a worse adder's slime! He thrusts
A scorching glare that burns in like a coal,
And fangs the writhing life that vainly trusts
Her charms exposed to move him! His control
Complete, a beast he gloats, extinguishing the soul!

XI.

The moving of an iron bolt below,
Harsh thro' the corridor grates on the ear!
Light footfalls follow cautiously and slow, —
Now pausing — dying out — they disappear,
And now returning, stealthily more near.
Ewald springs softly to her bolted door,
And still as statue leans in breathless fear;
Till, pale as moonbeams on her prison floor,   [more.
Her young cheeks turn, as nearer draw the steps once

XII.

The dusky shadows seem to glint and move —
The ghostly creatures of expectancy,
Wont mid such scenes in these dark halls to rove,
And perch around and gloat mysteriously!
Yet Ewald leans and listens tremblingly.
But now what pangs! — a hurried footstep lands
Without, a hasty hand thrusts in a key, —
The iron yields! a man before her stands! —   [hands!
She darts across her cell, she moans! she wrings her

XIII.

He follows up, — at each approach she flies —
She shrinks — she mutters and entreating stares!
The sullen walls drink up her fruitless cries,
While thus enraged the monster on her glares,
And with brute force to seize his prey prepares!
One pleading look to heav'n she wildly throws,
And sinks upon her couch still mutt'ring prayers ;
Then like a flying fury at him goes,
Flings wide her prison door and publishes her woes!

XIV.

So the caged bird goes struggling from the hand,
To beat and flutter 'gainst her wirery dome ;
And 'scapes at last, to leave her troubler stand
Astonished, as she gains her woody home!
How Ewald passed the night, and saved by whom,
No one may tell, but she was saved from shame,
And when my patient reader shall have come
To ponder well a vet'ran leader's name,
He may remember that to him belongs the fame.

XV.

Still on misfortune blindly moves her train!
We may not linger here; the time draws nigh,
Twasinta's wasted homes appeal in vain,
Palmecho sees his doom! Ah! must he die?
The lurid morn seems waiting in the sky,
As the avenger's mortal work proceeds!
Surely, if human acts are seen on high,
The bosom of angelic nature bleeds,
As yonder hangman to the death his victim leads!

XVI.

Lo! where Palmecho stoops within the gate,
How touching is his tender last farewell!
His child from him they cannot separate,
Tho' ruthless hands provoke the purpose fell!
A daughter's sweet affection who can tell?
A father's benediction how sublime,
When on his lips the words of parting dwell,
And he is pausing on the brink of time,
To lift his eyes towards a brighter, holier clime!

XVII.

Could scenes of bloodshed fill the eyes of death
With mischief too abhorrent, — could the pores
Of cruelty ooze drops, or his hot breath
Grow dull and bated — on the cypress shores
Where Ewald for her aged sire implores,
A cause is seen.   Lo! where yon scaffold stands
Gloomy above, while rock-watched Tampa roars!
Clench'd in despair behold her outstretched hands,
Whilst round her grimly press the war-stained soldier-
    bands!

XVIII.

Ah! doomed to die for shedding human blood,
He who has never caused a mortal pain!
But never martyr's faith more nobly stood
A sacrifice by tyrant madly slain!
Never did resignation less complain!
Stern looking on his executioner,
He pities him, nor hopes to pity gain;
When 'mid the throngs he hears his child demur,
And turns to rest a parent's loving gaze on her!

XIX.

"Thou last hope of my dotage, oh! my child;
Thou one green branch of age's withered tree,
I see thee shiv'ring in the tempest wild,
That tears thy parent trunk away from thee!
Ah! I could wish thou didst not mourn for me!
Then could I yearn to find the long, long sleep
That kisses down life's damp lids tranquilly
From all their sorrows! But thy courage keep —
The end may come at last, with joy for those who weep!"

XX.

Ah! there was Pathos on her very knees,
And chained Endurance pitying his child!
E'en Cruelty, red-handed's ill at ease
Where beauty pleads so tenderly and wild;
And to death's stroke old age stands reconciled. [spare!"
"Spare! spare my father! won't you! — won't you —
The daughter cries till vengeance is beguiled
From wanton haste, and seems for once to care,
And hold his doubtful breath at shrieks of wild despair!

XXI.

"My father! oh, my father! Do not bring
His guiltless hairs dishonored to the grave!
He did not — could not have done such a thing!
He never wronged a soul! — he never gave
A child offense! Oh! do but *this*, I crave! —
Be not in haste a good man's blood to shed!
Oh! spare! and I will be your willing slave
Till he who to the fatal rescue led
Shall show that by Palmecho's hand no soldier bled!

XXII.

A brawny guard the frantic pleader grasps,
To force her off, — she breaks away and flies
Thro' the grim throng, towards her father— clasps
His stooping neck, — upon his bosom lies,
And looking *cold* in her assailant's eyes,
Half hid in raven clouds of falling hair, —
"You *shall not!*— Oh! you *shall not! shall not!*" cries.
Ah! what a stroke for tragic art was there, —
Grief on his aged breast supporting young despair!

XXIII.

The spirits of the wood by Tampa seem
To sink their hidings into darker shade.
There lingers not the least reluctant beam
Amid the gloom that doth the scene pervade.
The scaffold specter-like, on high arrayed,
Looks down in grim rebuke.   A pause ensues,
A moment flies — another still delayed
Brings indecision, — when the leaders choose
To wait, and to secure Atlassa, Ewald use.

XXIV.

"Return them to their cells!" is the command;
"A fortnight hence shall be the time allowed,
And if Atlassa come not with his band,
Palmecho hangs!   And thus this Nation vowed!
Ah! could such be, when all the land was proud
And boastful of the policy of war,
That swept from over Florida the cloud
That brooded in destruction's gloom afar?
Was such majestic battle's only exemplar!

XXV.

Oh! Florida! how fair and yet how frail,
Thou daughter of the Sun, bereft, forlorn!
'Tis sad to hear thy exiled children's wail,
And hear thy empty fields in concert mourn,
While Rapine dwells where Peace did once sojourn!
'Tis sad that Ewald now in prison pines.
Ah! it were better to have ne'er been born!
But there is still a hope that ne'er resigns,   [joins.
And woman's heart is strong when this with courage

XXVI.

The moon was low on Tampa's quiet wave,
The drowsy camp was silent in the hill,
And patient earth was all composure, save,
A little while away, a night bird shrill
Trilling her throat was heard, when all was still.
A sentinel lone standing in the moon
Was all that might be seen of life, until
Beneath the prison walls there did commune
Twasinta's child and Abraham, the old Maroon.

XXVI.

Thus spoke the eager maid : " Oh! Abraham,
Be thou my message-bearing Angel! Fly!
Find out his camp! — inform him where I am —
Tell him his friend Palmecho's doomed to die, —
Tell him to come in haste, the time is nigh!
He is a warrior and a wary chief,
And keeps his guard, but tell him, somehow I
Am anxious that he *watch!* — be not too brief —
For harm to him will add calamity to grief!

XXVIII.

"Hint that the pomp and circumstance of war
Suggest strong body-guards and chosen men.
And let a truce flag, waving from afar,
Impose a friendly aspect; gathering then
His warriors well about him, wait, and when
The garrison comes out, be it declared
Who slew the guards in San Augustine's glen.
Then may Palmecho's life to me be spared,
And him to rescue, mankind know, Atlassa dared!"

XXIX.

Now, Abraham! if you have ever loved
A child — your own — or if you e'er did feel
A fount of sorrow in your bosom moved,
Turn not your ear from wildest grief's appeal!
Earth's last support to woman's trembling weal
Is faith in man! — then covenant with me —
While at the shrine of trust my soul shall kneel, —
Do covenant that thou wilt faithful be,   [thee!
And woman's prayers in heaven shall breathe a word for

XXX.

The brave old chief of peace and kindly deeds,
Lifted towards the moon his bronzed brow,
And pond'ring as a man who deeply heeds,
Uttered his answer carefully and low:
"Maiden, the stars are looking at me now, —
They oft have seen me, thro' the long, long past,
Going about for peace; and they will glow
As many witnesses, that, to the last,
The feet of Abraham, for good were ever fast.

XXXI.

" The cypress and the desert pine can tell
How often I have traveled night and day,
And in their shades what perils me befell,
From savage beasts infesting every way,
And scouts more savage that around me lay;
That I should falter now, 'twould seem too late, —
Trust me! is all that Abraham can say ! "
Thus ended, Ewald watched him from the gate,
Till lost from view within the moon-lit forests great.

XXXII.

Hail Florida! ye palmy forests hail !
Hail densest pines and fields of endless bloom!
'Twas sweet, I ween, in Apalachi's vale,
To wander forth in the deep foliage gloom,
Where the wide air was scarce of breathing room, —
To see the soft bananas drooping thro',
And the great dusky yellow orange loom
Mid languid leaves: Thus as the aspect grew
From change to change, the eye did fresh delights pursue.

XXXIII.

'Twas sweet to see the blossoms, many-hued,
Flush in the Summertide's luxuriant smile,
Soft shim'ring in the sunlight, half subdued
By great dense boughs of green.　'Twas sweet to while
The hours by fenceless paths for many a mile ;
To pause 'mid the great shades where the birds swung,
And follow fancy's pleased eye thro' each aisle,
To nymph abodes, the leafy haunts among;　[tongue.
Where hues had speech and fragrance wooed us with her

XXXIV.

Such scenes as these, the exile's pensive eye
Enjoyed with satisfaction deep and true.
The Seminole looked proud and dreamily,
Or musing walked, with scarcely more to do.
Surely there never was a happier view!
From town to town, mid groves and by the sea,
To Mickasukie and the great Wahoo;
The joyous scenes of Summer wild and free,
Lured Care to rest on Pleasure's lap continually.

XXXV.

Hark! in the troubled West what means this roar?
Like forests in a storm's tremendous glee,
Or like the waves on dread Atlantic's shore,
It rolls and breaks around Mickanopy!
Oh! what hath roused this angry human sea?
Why howls the waste in such unwonted throes?
What rends the bosom of tranquillity?
The loud, resistless onset of fierce foes,
Startles a peaceful land and breaks its deep repose!

XXXVI.

Lo! the fierce bands from distant solitudes,
And hasty scouts from Apalachi's side!
The mutt'ring foe is threading Tampa's woods,
With savage Creeks and loud-mouthed hounds allied;
Wide o'er the land his mounted patrols ride,
Thro' hommocks dark and forests dense they lead;
While burning villages afar descried,
Proclaim the bold incendiary's deed,
And make the heavens lurid where the hosts proceed!

XXXVII.

This is the conquest of the flow'ry land!
He who has earned the fame of many wars —
America's chief captain, in command,
Marshals his battle-hardened regulars !
Proud thro' the pine woods float the stripes and stars,
And restive steeds toward the onset neigh;
While, kindling recollections of his scars,
In his green haunts no longer to give way,
The Seminole looks forth, a hunted beast at bay!

XXXVIII.

Ah! 'tis the dreadful eve of battle now!
The low'ring storm of nations comes apace;
Deep clouds have settled on Destruction's brow,
And dismal thunders hem Atlassa's race!
Ah! what but valor stands in such a place?
Wives, children, and the old, all mounted wait
To fly at once, while in each warrior's face
The inwrought lines of deep, resentful hate
Betray that now resistance will be desperate.

XXXIX.

The threat'ning storm no longer holds its wrath,
The sanguine troops their stubborn foe engage;
While allied Creeks skulk 'round in every path,
Nefarious flankings, right and left to wage;
Torturing Desperation into rage,
And demon yells with roar of muskets blend:
But, rallying fierce upon the hommock's edge,
They who for homes and liberty contend,
As grim as *Hate* receive the troops and *on* them bend!

XL.

His fearless plume, lo! how Atlassa bears,
For deadly aiming guns a brilliant mark!
The erring bullet hisses at his ears,
But *heedless still* he walks a god; and hark!
His voice is clear! Loud o'er the battle dark
Its tones of magic urge his braves to fame
And deeds of daring! and the latest spark
Of ebbing life it kindles to a flame,
As each expiring warrior gasps his leader's name!

XLI.

Ah! ye who con the musty tomes of eld,
To watch the fabled scorpions of ire
Kindle the fatal wrath that mankind held
In mortal dread, behold this chief, in dire
And desp'rate conflict, build a deadlier fire
Around the rude homes of his tribal braves!
Tortured, the angry flames can not expire,
Each warrior like a fury now behaves, —   [slaves?
All like wild beasts *hunt* death! Ah! can such men be

XLII.

Furies imprisoned by infernal hate,
Where the hot irons circumvex their pains,
Surge not more fierce on Torture's brazen gate,
Nor writhe defiant more in blist'ring chains,
When, death inducing not, doth stream their veins;
Than surge and writhe these Seminoles beneath
The hail of angry lead that on them rains!
From tree and hommock *rushing* to the death,
They blanch grim slaughter's cheeks and drink his very
    breath!

XLIII.

Flying like wing'd madness on what they seeth,
They hand the foe within the dreadful breach!
Fastening him like torments with hungry teeth,
Till lifeless one shall sink, and sometimes each,
They hew down all within the tom'hawk's reach!
So fly infuriated hornets from their nests,
Upon assailants: Thus doth valor teach,
When roused to desperation's potent tests,
That "Liberty or Death," is one of God's behests!

XLIV.

Fierce Spirit of the Seminole! what fate
Can tame thy warring sons upon the field!
I see them for a Nation's strength *too* great —
Outnumbered and outarmed they *will not* yield!
Till by the darkness they are well concealed,
They hold an army back and guard their dead;
Thus shall their immortality be sealed,
The bravest of the brave, to victory led,
By one whose plume would honor e'en a Bruce's head!

XLV.

Down to the end of time be it proclaimed!
Up to the skies of fame let it be rung!
Wherever valor's sacrifice is named,
Whenever plaudits fire the human tongue;
Or by sweet strings expressed, or mortals sung,
Let it go forth, and let mankind attest,
That, Seminoles and exiles, old and young,
Upon the bosom of their country prest;
By valiant deeds are shrined in ev'ry patriot breast!

XLVI.

Thro' the dead desolation of the past,
The eye of Freedom searches not in vain,
For her surviving shrines, — the pomp and blast
Of might and red Dominion, could attain
To manacling the world's limbs and its brain;
But Freedom's sons must dwell unknown, — apart —
Or wander hopeless, in Contempt's sad plain;
Yet ever, and anon, some giant heart, —
Some prince of thought, a revolution's tide would start.

XLVII.

Some Bruce or Tell, who drank the mountain breath
Of Freedom, and arose to meet her morn;
Some Brown or Lovejoy, whose contempt of death,
Was of the sacred love of Freedom born, —
Whose mentioned dust would shame the lips of scorn!
Some Jefferson, the Knight of Justice fair,
Whose thoughts the brow of ages still adorn;
And whose brave lance of independence rare,
Could thrust base Superstition in her dragon lair!

XLVIII.

Or some Atlassa, who could call his braves
To turfy beds of glory in the dell,
Or vict'ry o'er those who would make them slaves! —
But for such men the wide earth were a hell,
Where vampire priests and kingly vultures fell,
Plucking the fleshless bones of human woe
Would perch thro' time! and in the waste and spell
Of nniversal carnage, loud or low,
The owls of Superstition would forever go.

XLIX.

The enthusiasts' torch that lit their beacon fires
From Plymouth's Sea to cold Ontario's coasts,
Shone farther than the ken of Pilgrim sires,
In their brief time surveyed :   The sturdy hosts
That throated Tyranny and scorned his boasts,
Knew not that on this continent of streams, —
Of endless summers and eternal frosts —
'Mid first-born woods, the light of Freedom beams
On sovran Nature's lap, inducing patriot dreams!

L.

They saw, but " comprehended not the light " —
Colonial life was but a prophecy —
They kindled dimly in an unknown hight,
But could no more — and paused there trustingly,
Till sons explored the ages then *to be*.
And while in silence and eternal dust
They sleep beneath the standard they left free,
A proud Republic — their pathetic trust —
Fraternal hands embellish, and forever must!

LI.

And tho' 'tis sad, in truth it must be said,
They died for Freedom and for *slavery* too!
How noble and *ignoble* are our dead,
How recreant to right, and yet how true!
But o'er a century's historic view,
The valiant Seminole we proudly see ;
He died for *Freedom;* and the trembling few
Who fled to Florida his wards to be,
He elevated into freemen's dignity!

LII.

He could not be enslaved — would not enslave
The meanest exile that his friendship sued,
Brave for himself, defending others brave, —
The matchless hero of his time he stood,
His noble heart with freedom's love imbued,
The strong apostle of Humanity!
'Mid forests wild and habitations rude,
He made his bed of glory by the sea;
The friend of Florida and man, there let him be!

LIII.

Upon the proud front let Atlassa stand,
Night in the everglades is friendly now.
The foe retires and darkness is at hand,
And seems to listen to the voices low
Of warriors round their chief, whose valiant brow
Is heavy with the horrors of the day!
Upon the turf the wounded in a row,
Painful but silent, for attention lay, —
The dead to Apalachi's shores are borne away.

LIV.

The war is ended, let the victor rest!
His brave blood seals the title of his fame.
His fair land deems him worthy of her breast,
Historic truth embalms his warlike name,
While hero temples well admit his claim!
And when the epic muse shall cast around,
A theme to kindle valor into flame,
Where Florida's soft palms shade many a mound,
By Mickasukie and the sea, will *e'er* be found.

LV.

Oh! inexorable, oh! righteous Time,
Thy mist-dispersing light o'er us roll on!
Let thy just beams invest the Sunny Clime,
And bring the truth up from the ages gone!
Oh! we are happy as we stand upon
The summit of a century, and view
How hist'ry pales where thy broad beams have shone!
Thou dread revealer of the old and new,
Inevitable are thy judgments, just and true!

CANTO IV.

I.

Gazing upon the toiling seas,
In gloomy rows the silent captives sate;
And as the ship rode off before the breeze,
They murmured not, though all disconsolate;
But mournful seemed, and joined to meditate, —
Each other to regard with patient sighs,
And gather courage up to hope and wait;
Still looking back, with sad, reluctant eyes,
To bid a last adieu to Florida's blue skies!

II.

Those who had counselled Tampa's sons of old,
Now lift their drooping faces from their hands;
And those who had done battle stern and bold, —
Fierce sons of Seminole and exile bands, —
Look up as in their midst Atlassa stands.
Shorewards his arms in heavy irons stretch,
And while his mien a silence deep commands,
His fiery glance inspires the veriest wretch,
For all well know that he's for mortal foe a match!

III.

Full well they know the perfidy and guile,
By which at Tampa, they in chains were held.
The insult to a flag of truce, so vile,
Astounded all, and in each bosom swelled,
A bitter, mute despondency. Compelled
To charge themselves with lack of wariness,
They felt that they from homes were self-expelled;
So, sighs alone, their feelings could express,
As their attentive ear drank down their chief's address.

IV.

"My native Florida! adieu! adieu!
I'm looking at the last pine on thy shore!
Soon other climes must come upon my view,
And thy sweet landscapes meet my eyes no more!
Oh! Florida! hear now thy son implore!
In thy fair bosom still remember me;
And while the billows shall between us roar,
Or thy smooth sands shall hear a lisping sea,
Let these my latest vows revive and dwell in thee!

V.

"I go in chains, but not a pining slave;
Injured but conquered not, I still go free!
And yet, ye seats by Mickasukie's wave,
How sad it is that I must *thus* leave thee!
'Twas in thy shades I hoped my grave might be.
When Peace had come to spread her happy reign.
Where sleep the prophet-sires of liberty,
I proudly deemed that comrades should have lain
My weary dust in rest unbroken to remain!

VI.

"Ye pines whose whisper's lulled thy child to rest,
And whose hoarse anthems nerved him in the fray,
How slept thy shades on Mickasukie's breast,
How crept they from the threshold of the day! —
From such sweet scenes I'll soon be far away!
And Apalachi, parted now from me,
No words can utter what my heart would say! —
But while thy pining shores no more I see,
In his far home, Atlassa still will think of thee!"

VII.

The chieftain speaks no more, but still doth gaze
Till Florida is gone and all is sea.
With every canvas breathing, sailors raise
Their outward shouts, and sing right merrily
To the dark wave's responsive melody:
But hark! what groans now fill the heedless wind!
The captive can his home no longer see;
So sinks in unsupported grief the mind,   [hind!
When exiles dragged away, must leave their hearts be-

VIII.

Atlassa sees those who, whilom could look
Upon him with a hope of sure redress;
And feelings that e'en *his* heart cannot brook,
Damp his averted eyes, and thoughts that press
Like flame, he feels and cannot half express.
There are his comrades in long bloody wars;
Their lips are still — their looks speak none the less, —
Their maimed limbs, and their faces deep with scars,
Are the dumb eloquence which tells the wrong that mars.

IX.

There is a time when speech is all too frail,
There is a *place* where silence speaks the most:
What is the word to paint a human wail,
Or how heroic, *speak* where all is lost!
He who wears shackles mid his shackled host,
Shows valor's *steel* to sturdily behave,
For life is Freedom's last and *real* cost,
And so, the *last* resistance of the brave,
Is that stern silence which to chains prefers grave.

X.

Full well the patient exile knows his chief,
Full well the Seminole regards his mien ;
For to look on him is a strange relief
To those who *with* him, other times have seen,
Ah ! they remember *well* what he hath been, —
How readily he sprang to meet the foe !
Bearing misfortunes manfully serene,
They see him now, and trust that he may know
The way of their deliv'rance, and direct the blow.

XI.

Still sing the sailors 'mid their masts and spars,
All heedless of a captive's sighs aboard !
In truth 'tis a good time for jolly tars —
The heaving canvas hastens them toward
Their haven, and sea-omens good afford
Continuous presages of a fair sail;
While sportive fancy kens ahead to hoard
The dance, and sparkling draught that shall regale,
When they the Crescent City's busy port shall hail.

XII.

How near may men be, yet how far apart,
If what lies all unuttered were but told!
How changed is all the province of the heart,
When different men the selfsame sights behold!
To one the skies may glow in dusts of gold,
Sprinkled by hands of promise, while the same
To others like the book of Doom unrolled,
May doleful seem, — toned with the lurid flame [name.
That lights the ruins and gloom of mishaps dread to

XIII.

Atlassa leans, stern looking on his chains,
All else unheeding till a touch he feels, —
Before him stands the soldier-porting Gaines,
His lifted hat the veteran-brow reveals.
With wars acquainted, nought his mien conceals ;
Meeting the chief as brave men meet the brave,
A glance of mutual admiration seals
The friendliness with which they each behave :
" Unbind him," thunders he, "Atlassa is no slave ! "

XIV.

' I've thrown away my rifle," cries the chief,
" I hold a brave hand, we shall now be friends ! "
The soldier answers and his words were brief ; —
" Only in battle foes, in peace strife ends.
In arms, your conduct to mankind commends
You as a warrior, honorable — *true*.
And now the General in command extends
The hand of high fraternity to you, —
Believe me, sir, and this with heartfelt pride I do."

XV.

Straightening to all his hight, the vet'ran Gaines,
With martial pride investing his high brow,
The signal gives, — a band, discoursing strains
Enliv'ning, starts — and expectancy now
Stands tiptoe.   Seaman at the stern and prow,
And high amid the rigging, hush and wait ! —
Palmecho is unchained and from below,
Totters up in a poor unsteady gait —
The pathos of an old man borne from sorrow's weight!

XVI.

There was a hush upon the swelling wave,
The spirit of the waters seemed to be
A silent noticer.   The full sails gave
A flutter short and listened breathlessly;
The mews came nearer from the open sea,
And over all there was a deep'ning spell,
Till trumpets flourished loud and suddenly,
And then sweet strains again commenced to swell,
When Ewald sprang and on her chieftain's bosom fell.

XVII.

Ewald the princess of the sunny isle,
Ewald the idol of Twasinta's vale, —
The fascinating beauty, who, erwhile
A captive pined, in long suspense grown pale, —
Not now less beautiful, but much more frail,
Her dark unconquered eyes still claim their reign,
Lovely in triumph ! no weak sob or wail
Escape her lips, or word unmeet and vain ;
She simply looks a queen, restored to realms again !

XVIII.

The dark wave smiled, the sails flapped swifter on,
The mews were off about their foam intent ;
And e'en the vet'ran Gaines was up and gone,
When o'er Ewald the silent chieftain leant ;
Too well *he* knew what such reunions meant !
Ah ! who could rudely linger on the scene,
When arms reluctant pressed by love consent,
And lips like rose-buds with their dews between, [been
Their dainty sweets yield to the touch ?   It would have

XIX.

A sacrilege polluting e'en the sea!
Not Jonah's disobedience could have stirred
The Ocean gods to wrath more suddenly.
This scene in Neptune's realms, was, in a word,
A part, in Bliss Regained, by him preferred
Before the patrons of the wave, to show
That e'en love's *whispers* in the deep are heard —
That her entrancings charm the tides that flow,
And please the pow'rs that reign invincibly below.

XX.

Ye who are scornful of an injured race, —
Who boast thy fellow mortal to despise,
Look now on war-worn Gaines' valiant face,
Look in the glorious old commander's eyes,
Gaze, as on Ewald's neck his proud hand lies,
See how *her* sweet hand nestles there in his ;
Now with coy glances, see, she deftly tries
And wins the admiring smile which ever gi'es
Woman a pleasure true and man's best treasure is.

XXI.

Now ask the vet'ran — but his fiery eye
Is on you! Look! Draw near! Stand in its blaze
And let it scorch! — Approach him — there! ask " Why,
Our leader, why, Sir, bring us the disgrace
Which must attach to fawning Ewald's race ? "
Imagine that he answers! — hold! now go,
Make haste, forsooth! hide thy repugnant face
Till thou art cured! and after this be slow   [know.
To stretch thy curious neck life's nobler springs to

XXII.

But we must hasten to a foreign shore, —
To ancient Santa Rosa lift thine eyes ;
There the worn exiles, free at last, explore
The plain that by no slave polluted lies
Beneath the peaceful blue of Mexic's skies ;
There may they taste their freedom so well won,
Surrounded by their happy families ;
There may rejoice to find their struggles done,
And Plenty's benedictions close what wars begun.

XXIII.

Where the wild cactus lifts its thorny stem,
And sleepily endures the day-long heat,
A free and fruitful clime inviteth them
To rest their whilom weary, wand'ring feet.
Oh! how inspiriting the prospect sweet
That now expands upon the open gaze!
Above them yet their tropic branches meet,
The fruit boughs hang in luscious golden maze,   [lays.
And winds are burdened with their native wood-land

XXIV.

Here the clear stream holds in its peaceful brim
Such quiet shadows as to them recall
The scenes of Mickasukie's forests dim ;
And, mindful still of what did them befall,
Though not cast down, they rise up after all,
And here commence the dream of life again.
Soon cheerful hearths unite their fam'lies small,
The husbandman leads up his joyous train,
And pleasant farms extend wide o'er the vocal plain.

XXV.

There stands Atlassa 'mid his hopeful few,
The future contemplates and looks before.
The battle storm that erst around him drew
Them to defend their wasted land is o'er.
And now lamenting not his native shore,
He rises still as one born to command,
And challenge comrade's courage tried once more.
He waves the signal of his gifted hand,
And valiantly they go to subjugate the land.

XXVI.

He led them forth of old, they knew not where,
He followed with them o'er the mournful wave;
They halted in the wilderness, and there
The human hunter waited to enslave, —
He stepped to front again their leader brave,
And when the foe came on with haughty stride,
A death blow to his insolence he gave:
Then came the weary march, thro' forests wide,
Till they were safe beyond the Rio Grande's tide.

XXVII.

There, mourning not, they toil and hope again, —
They look not back, their sodden cheeks are dry;
And yet, I ween, there is an inward pain
To those whose kindred all unnoticed lie
Beneath the sad sun of a foreign sky.
The South wind whispers to them o'er the wave,
And dampness is, perhaps, come in some's eye
Who thinks of a dear, well-remembered grave;
But all to mourn are too long suffering and too brave.

XXXVIII.

Since he who looks upon a glorious day
Expiring on the threshold of the West,
Must breathe a thoughtful wish to be away ;
And feel within him dying unexprest
The seer-voiced longings of the heart's unrest ;
May we not trust that, in the evermore,
A friendlier clime awaits the pensive breast ;
May we not hope to reach a farther shore,
And catch the billows listing where they cease to roar ?

XXIX.

Oh ! must it ever come that earth shall be
A sable field of barrenness ?   A waste
Of hollow sounds ?   Must fruitless nature see
Her seasons end ?   And sunless days — the last —
Roll sightless on mid desolations vast ?
Must Time in silence view her broken urn,
Or sit to brood upon an empty Past ?
Bereft of years, must she a widow mourn,
And to her childless breast will joy no more return ?

XXX.

And since there is, as hope is prone to sing,
A " Happy Land," why say " far, far away ? "
May not the restful soul be lingering
Still near its mansion of deserted clay ?
The unembodied spirit, why not say,
By matter all unhindered, is at home ;
Whether delighted round the earth to stray,
Or in a farther universe to roam, —
A guest of future worlds, — then back at times to come !

XXXI.

If conscious life about the earth might stroll,
A child of Reason still, it then were sweet
To think on a Republic of the soul —
Community of Spirits — where *lives* meet
To walk the earth they've known, with joyous feet,
Unharrowed by abysmal thoughts of Death;
Reason would then hold her delightful seat,
And tho' what's mortal, but a mist, a breath,
Were passed away, *life* still would be her "shibboleth."

XXXII.

'Twere sweet to live, if cherishing the trust
That life *itself* doth from the flesh-life spring, —
That what survives affection's tender dust
Is *this* existence, *only* brightening
With azure grace and an immortal wing!
Then might we hope to *feel* as we have *felt*,
And *know* the subtle shadow wavering
Between the *where* we *may* dwell and have dwelt;
Then might we realize that not in vain we've knelt.

XXXIII.

If then, this be, how sweet the pleasing dream, —
When life had filled its shadow and its shine, —
That led the savage by his dark-wood stream,
To seek a heaven beneath his leafy shrine!
In pathos sweet and tenderness divine,
This solace for the poorest heart pleads:
When this life o'er her empty urn shall pine,
She sit to mourn not in eternal weeds;
But, part the shade into the shine that *there* succeeds.

XXXIV.

Those who have labored up dogmatic Blancs
To freeze on horrid crags, or dash below
Into some mangling chasm did leave the banks
And shades of safety in the plain, to know,
Only too late, that such hights can but show
Distances too sublime by far to reach, —
Only too late, that tend'rest comforts grow
Where love's sweet whispers cluster round, to teach
The dear humanity that they disdained to preach.

XXXV.

Who can ascend against Thy awful brow,
Omnipotence! About Thee Thou dost gird
The elements! Thine avalanches flow
Down the incomputable years! and heard
Eternally comes forth Thy Sovran Word,
To warn man back! Thy presence who can bear?
E'en of old in mountains thou appeared,
And from thine upper worlds man Thee did hear,
And quake to stand in clouds of an unmortal fear!

XXXVI.

Thou warnest me the mortal task to shun,
Of tempting thy dread paths above to find.
Stern, silent, incomprehensible One!
Thou risest boundlessly above the mind!
But here below thou hast for love entwined
An altar with the leaf of life, and bloom,
Round which, pathetic human tendrils bind
The off'rings of our hands. May its perfume
Exhale in all the earth, as freedom's fires consume!

XXXVII.

But we have wandered: If the Seminole
May ever reach again his native shore,
How sweet to think of his unhindered soul
Revisiting the scenes he loved before!
But if the hope offend we say no more:
We leave him in his Mexic home at rest,
And still may *dream* that he shall yes pass o'er
The dimpling waves of Mickasukie's breast,
Yet press the flow'ry brinks, that he before has prest!

XXXVIII.

The exiles came unto an ancient well, —
Atlassa sat and Ewald by him stood,
While golden glories of the sunset, fell
Like dreams of heav'n on Santa Rosa's wood.
A shim'ring silence filled the solitude.
There was no time for speech. Palmecho moaned
For joy, and wept, and their responses rude,
With feelings deep and weirdly undertoned,
The warriors gave, still gazing on the earth peace-zoned.

XXXIX.

Oh! God! in all Thy glorious works, Thy praise
Is mightiest mid the hosts of Liberty!
She leads mankind in devious unknown ways,
And sounds her timbrels o'er a conquered sea,
While vocal mountains catch the rising glee!
And, where afar her patient children roam,
The desert wakes to join their jubilee!
They pass or rest, despising what may come;
Only to dwell with thee, the wide world is their home.

XL.

Hail! home of exiles and of Seminoles!
Hail! Mexico, thou weak but goodly land!
The Day of Freedom onward grandly rolls,
And thou shalt yet receive the greeting hand
Of her, who once did like a vulture stand,
To gorge upon thy sons by slave power slain!
The world's respect, ere long thou shalt command;
And when the hosts of Freedom come amain; [plain!
Thy sons shall join their shouts ascending from the

XLI.

Those who once came upon thee with the sword,
Are coming now with pruning hooks and plows;
And plains, once trampled by the spoiler's horde,
Are green with fields, and sweet with fruitful boughs.
Awake thou ebon maid! awake! arouse!!
Throw wide thy gates! unlock thy treasures now!
The proud cause of humanity espouse;
And from thy miser-clutching hills shall flow
The wealth that yet must glitter in thy sunny brow!

XLII.

Rise from thy ancient mounds! cells of the dead,
Of whom e'en Legend recollects no tale;
Presumption *only*, sees the life they led
In squalid hut, and still, unplanted dale:
And even *she* is sad to lift the veil!
Oh! what must they have been! Oh! how expire
And on the ears of Time leave not a wail?
In all the past, there smokes no altar fire —
To what renown *could* such a stupid race aspire!

XLIII.

And yet may lowly joys have there been born,
Rude tho' the scenes 'mid which her patrons met.
The sheep boy's carol and the mountain horn,
And merry note of pipe or flageolet,
May well be deemed the things we can't forget;
And these may there have soothed the rustic's ear,
Still, still it comes, unceasing with regret,
That there remains no lingering mark of cheer —
That not a solitary annal doth appear.

XLIV.

We leave thee with thy guests, thou sunny maid!
The daughter of Twasinta dwells with thee;
The chief of Tampa and the everglade
Is with her, and will strive to keep thee free.
Rise thou into a nation's dignity,
And freedom's acclamations spread around!
As Rio Grande rolls down to the sea,
Let the omnific waters catch the sound,
"A queen of beauty in the West is Mexic crowned!"

XLV.

Farewell, thy guests! The light is almost gone
That kindled for them in the everglades!
In all our shores the day of slavery's done.
Midst the wild freedom of our mighty shades,
Now, every man whose soul the hope pervades
Of life, and liberty, and happiness,
May join with Sovran Labor's plows and spades,
And jocund axes in the wilderness,
To dig and hew away primeval want's fortress.

XLVI.

Who finds *this* country *now*, exulting finds
That nature sounds the anthems of the free, —
The boundless prairie swept by restless winds,
Great forests shouting on tumultuously,
Rivers that send their greetings to the sea,
Peace-loving vales, where weed-brimmed waters run,
Broad lakes, whose shade-fringed margins lisp their glee,
Mountains, that prop their green heights in the sun,
And herded slopes that winter never looks upon!

XLVII.

Priestcraft and Tyranny must not unchain
The mind and limb of man and send him here;
Or they will never see their dupe again,
So soon 'mong freemen will he disappear.
The sights to make him free are everywhere:
He can not see the farmer tilling corn,
And whistling at his plow, as blithe and clear
As lark or linnet in the dew-sprent morn,
And not feel freedom's wishes in him being born.

XLVIII.

He can not wander in our roads, or stay
Beneath our shades unmoved by what he sees, —
The full ripe orchard by his dusty way,
Busy with children and alive with bees;
The cool spring underneath the green oak trees;
The cider mill a going merrily,
And farmer looking on in his brown ease, —
He can not, seeing these, but long to be
A sovereign, gathering gold crowns from the appletree.

XLIX.

This is a land of free limb and free thought —
Freedom for *all*, home-keeping or abroad, —
Here man is all unhindered, as he ought,
Dreading no priest's rebuke, no despot's nod,
In high respect of Right, the friend of God!
Sole sovereign of himself, by nature throned,
Planting his titles n the royal sod,
He spreads his reign were labor's might is owned,
And harvests revenues for which no subject groaned.

L.

The veriest serf, whose shiv'ring manhood hears
Niagara's astounding waters fall,
Must find that awe of man there disappears
In mists of infinite spray: He can not call
His monarch's name and feel its spell and thrall;
For human might is swept off in the gaze
And awe of One Sublime Stupendous *All!*
And nought survives except the soul to raise
To one great God a whisper of deep, sincere praise!

LI.

Thus ends my lay: Reluctantly I leave
Atlassa and his sweet-eyed Southern maid;
Palmecho, too, with whom I much did grieve,
I turn from sadly!   Could they but have stayed
Beneath their "vines and fig trees," not afraid!
Yet by their Santa Rosa let them dwell,
Rejoicing in their freedom, long delayed!
And while my heart's untrained emotions swell,
Once more I turn to gaze and sigh: farewell! farewell!